MW00389117

MAKER TO MANUFACTURER

*Organizing and Running Your
Studio Using Tips and Tricks From
the Factory Floor*

Kate Jakubas

Julie,
Wishing you business success
and a clean studio

Kate

Maker to Manufacturer: Organizing and Running Your Studio Using Tips and Tricks from the Factory Floor
Copyright © 2019 by Kate Jakubas. All Rights Reserved.

All rights reserved. No part of this book may be reproduced in any form or by any electronic or mechanical means including information storage and retrieval systems, without permission in writing from the author. The only exception is by a reviewer, who may quote short excerpts in a review.

This book contains information obtained from authentic and highly regarded sources. Reasonable efforts have been made to ensure the accuracy and applicability of this information for the purposes cited. However, the information presented is without warranty, express or implied.

Kate Jakubas
Visit my website at www.makertomanufacturer.com

Printed in the United States of America

Fulton Street Press

ISBN- 978-0-578-50104-8

Toolbox for improvement
Reduce and/or eliminate waste
5S — SORT, Set in order, Shine, Standardize, Sustain
purge   place for   clean,   MAKE IT A   keep
Kanban - Bins everything   style   HABIT   improving
                           substance
Stream Maps
Spaghetti Diagrams (floor diagrams)

Run your studio using Pull System, + Bins Kanban
Eliminating the endless to-do list.

Pull System: start with the customer. Do everything because your customer demands it.

Do not continue to make more product without your customers order.

BINS — auto Pilot for production.
Empty bin is my to-Do list.
BIN SIZE & NUMBER
How much fits in each Bin. Start with a single batch size.
Quantity
S: Sales
T Time
B # of Bins.

Bins
Stuff off floor
furniture movers
Buy another gar[...]

Author's Preface

You work hard to make an amazing product for your customers. When you need help, there are countless guides to help you refine branding and marketing, sales, and accounting. Your own (craft beer, jewelry, or cosmetics) industry even has guides and groups to help you refine your product designs and recipes. But until now, there has not been a guide to help you in running your studio space using the best practices of lean manufacturing. After working at factories around the USA and internationally, I have adopted common practices of lean manufacturing to create this guide designed specifically for small studios. Large companies have dedicated teams and use expensive consulting resources to improve their operations – now you can use these same practices to make your studio run like the world's most efficient factories.

Book Overview

Section 1 is about finding and getting your studio set up: optimizing your home studio or establishing one outside of your home.

Section 2 is about organizing your space: keeping it clean and orderly so you can make great product.

Section 3 is about running your space: buying materials, holding onto inventory, creating products, and then getting them out the door to your customers.

Start with 2 Bins $b = 1 + ($ $)$

Bigger Space?
Bigger Equipment? *Doesn't need to be SOAP SPECIFIC!*
Buy in Bulk? *Buy as little as possible. Set up delivery every day.*
Ties up cash, space.   *overhead*
Charge more for your products? Reduce costs labor, material

Myths 5

BUY LIQUID LYE in Drums. Chemical Suppliers
Sealer Chemicals— 50% by weight caustic soda
solution

CONTENTS

SECTION ONE: FINDING AND SETTING UP YOUR STUDIO

CHAPTER 1 – FINDING YOUR STUDIO SPACE

Will you make product at home or in an outside space? Finding a dedicated studio space for your business. Things to consider when developing your list of requirements. Looking for and negotiating a lease.

WHY HAVE A DEDICATED STUDIO?

Starting your business from the garage or basement is a grand tradition (ask Microsoft, Google, or almost any beer brewery). If your current at-home space is working well for you, stay there for the cost and convenience advantages.

Shared Spaces

After outgrowing your at-home space and before having your own studio, you may be able to rent commercial space by the hour in a shared kitchen or workshop in your area. These spaces have existing equipment and are geared toward a specific industry, such as food preparation or woodworking. Depending on your needs, you may be able to use them for your product as well: cosmetics can be made in a kitchen, for example, and artists and metalworkers can fit into a woodshop environment.

Your Own Studio

As you grow, one or more of the following things may contribute to your need for a new, dedicated studio location:

1. **Lack of space.** If your business is taking over your living space, it may be time to move out.
2. **Difficulties with zoning restrictions.** There are zoning rules you may not be following or didn't investigate when you first got started. Your home may not be a legally viable production site.
3. **Insurance requirements.** To properly insure both your home and business, you often need to have separate spaces.
4. **Truck delivery and pickup access.** Loading docks and truck bays make supplier deliveries easier, and some suppliers don't deliver to residential addresses.
5. **Customer and employee traffic.** A dedicated space keeps customers and employees out of your family's area and vice versa.

LOOKING FOR YOUR NEW SPACE

Commercial Versus Industrial

When moving from a residential space into a dedicated facility for your operations, you'll see the terms "commercial" and "industrial." They are not interchangeable; make sure you understand the local definitions and which designation is appropriate for what you need.

Typically, commercial space is for offices, stores, and restaurants, while industrial space typically is for manufacturing and warehousing. If you plan to have a combination of a storefront and manufacturing facility, pay extra attention to the uses allowed in each space you consider.

Starting Your Search

Finding and moving into an industrial space takes time. It's never too early to start keeping an eye on available properties in your area. Once you're ready and have a list of requirements for your space, it may still take a few months to negotiate a lease and finalize your move. The more flexible you are with timing, the better options you have when deciding whether open properties are the right fit for you. Begin by searching online for available properties to get an idea of the sizes and prices in your area. Loopnet.com and other industrial listings give you an idea of the sizes and costs of available properties. Although it's possible to purchase your space, most growing businesses opt for leasing. This book focuses only on leasing.

Example Property Search

Using Loopnet.com, I searched for industrial properties available for lease near the city of Rockford, IL. Sixteen available properties were listed, two of which were less than 10,000 square feet. Doing further research into all the available properties and visiting the areas in person will show you the industrially zoned areas nearby. A driving tour near listed properties gives you a chance to note the names of the real estate brokers or notice "for lease" signs on nearby properties. Existing businesses in the area may have extra space, which you can sublease.

Professionals Can Help

To protect yourself legally, find a real estate lawyer to look over any lease before you sign it; this is done for a flat or hourly fee. Having an attorney read your lease is a fast way to gain some protection, and the attorney can advise you of additional protections to request or items to add in an addendum to your lease, if needed.

You also can work with an industrial/commercial realtor to help you find the appropriate space. Just like a residential realtor, an industrial/commercial realtor helps you understand the general costs and amenities in your area, and advises you on what properties may be a good fit for your business. Typically landlords pay the realtors, so there is no cost to you.

REQUIREMENTS FOR YOUR NEW SPACE

Creating Your List of Requirements

Creating a list of must-haves and nice-to-haves will narrow your search and help you avoid getting stuck in an inappropriate space because of an appealing feature that's not needed. Your list of must-haves will be particular to you but probably will include the total square footage you need (see more on this in Chapter 2), a general location, required amenities such as in-unit water, and maximum total monthly cost. Use Table 1-1 to guide you in considering different features of a potential space. Make notes on any must-have and nice-to-have features for your own list, which you'll use to compare available properties.

Table 1-1. Features of an Industrial Facility

Category	Feature	Must Have	Nice to Have
Overall	Monthly cost	Maximum: ____	Target: ____
	Total square footage	Minimum: ____	Target: ____
	Zoning		
Facilities	Floors: type, ease of cleaning		
	Walls: type, noise reduction		
	Allowable floor loading weight		
	Electricity: voltage, outlet access		
	Lighting: efficiency, type of fixtures		
	Water: plumbing features and access		
	Plumbing/sewage: wastewater options		
	Windows: fresh air available, screens, light		
	Ceiling height		
	Climate control: heat, humidity, cooling, fans		

Table 1-1, continued

Category	Feature	Must Have	Nice to Have
Safety and Security	Fire alarms		
	Fire sprinklers		
	Security of doors and windows		
	Security cameras		
	Access restriction: keys, cards		
	Ventilation: fume hoods, exhaust systems		
Access	Bathrooms: location		
	Mail: mailroom access and location		
	Parking and public transportation		
	Stairs/elevators and pedestrian access		
	Loading dock for deliveries and shipments		
	Public-accessible area for tastings or retail		
	Public way access and foot traffic		
Other	Good manufacturing practice (GMP) needs		
	Other certification (organic, etc.) issues		
	Pest control		
	Ease of cleaning		
	Noise		
	Neighbors		
	Other:		

Your Comparison List

After determining your must-haves and nice-to-haves, create a checklist to take with you when looking at available properties. Comparing different spaces based on the important features will narrow your search and help you avoid deciding based on unimportant features.

Table 1-2. Example Space Comparison List

	Feature	Space A	Space B
Must Have	Total square footage over 2,000	Yes	Yes
	Loading dock access	Yes	Yes
	Within 20 miles of home	Yes	Yes
	Zoned for both production and warehousing	Yes	Yes
Nice to Have	First floor unit	Yes	No; third
	Concrete floors with floor drain	No	No
	Separate office area	No	No
	Package service in building	Front desk	Downstairs
Other Features to Note	Transportation notes	Parking lot	On bus line, street parking
	Bathrooms	Same floor	Same floor
	Public way access and foot traffic	OK	OK
	Access restriction: keys, cards	Keys	Keys
	Monthly rental cost	$4,000	$2,500
Further Notes		Same building as Sunshine Designs	Includes option to expand

Questions for Your Landlord or Leasing Agent

When you tour a space that may be a good fit for your new studio, here are some typical questions to ask to make sure you understand the main features of renting that property:

1. **Can I see a copy of a pro forma lease?** "Pro forma" means an advanced or expected copy, without particular information provided. A pro forma lease may not contain the exact details of your space (such as square footage and rental cost) but covers the main functions of the building, such as payment schedule and tenant and landlord responsibilities, for example. Reading it likely will answer many of the other questions below.

2. **What is the length of the lease?** Typical industrial spaces are for a 10-year term. Shorter leases are favorable for a growing business that may need to upgrade or is uncertain about future needs.

3. **What insurance coverage will I need?** The landlord may require a certain amount and type of insurance coverage, such as accident liability coverage for the premises. This would be in addition to any insurance you already need, such as product liability.

4. **Who pays for utilities: electric/water/gas?** You may need to manage your own service with utility providers, or pay a certain percentage of the total building costs. Make sure it's clear whether you pay an actual amount used or a percentage, and ask to see past bills for the space you are viewing to predict future utility costs.

5. **Who is responsible for maintenance?** Maintenance includes: snow removal, landscaping, recycling collection, landfill/refuse pickup, door security, plumbing, lighting, HVAC, equipment repairs, and regular cleaning, for example.

6. **Will the space be built to suit my needs?** If you need to install plumbing fixtures, lighting, flooring, walls, or other construction, the building may handle this for you, offer you a credit toward build-out, or leave you to pay for and manage the build-out yourself.

7. **What equipment is available for my use?** Security systems, loading dock equipment, freight elevators, forklifts, pallet jacks, ladders, and tools may be needed occasionally or regularly. Will you need to

provide your own equipment or can you use items owned by the landlord or neighbors?

8. **Will my rent stay the same or increase during my lease period?** If the rent does not stay the same for the entire lease, you should know the amount of increase per year or the total allowable amount of increase.

9. **Will I be able to renew my lease after the lease period ends?** Having the right of first refusal against other tenants interested in your space can help you plan for the long term.

10. **Can you—or I—end my lease early?** There should be conditions laid out to allow for ending the lease early. If you have an unexpected surge or stop in business and need to leave, you may be able to end your lease by paying a penalty or finding a sublessee. If your building is sold, your landlord may reserve the right to terminate your lease with a certain amount of notice.

11. **Can I expand my business footprint under the terms of this lease?** Your landlord may allow you to add additional space to your lease or move to a larger space owned by the same company.

12. **Can I sublease my space to another business?** If you aren't using your entire space, reduce costs by bringing in another business or renting storage space to another business.

13. **Who are the neighbors?** Nearby business operations can help—or hurt—yours. A large retail space may draw in customers. Loud or smelly operations may interfere with your operations or drive away your customers.

14. **Is there a co-tenancy clause?** For retail locations, if a large anchor tenant moves out, your business will be affected and you should be able to renegotiate your lease terms.

15. **Is there an exclusivity clause?** If you are opening a tasting room or retail storefront and need to avoid competitors close by, make sure your landlord will agree to not renting to certain similar businesses.

16. **What happens if the landlord is not able to meet the obligations in the lease?** If your landlord dies or declares bankruptcy, how will their responsibilities, such as maintenance, be handled? Your local bankruptcy code will have some information about this (most

obligations will cease, so you may get stuck handling things such as utilities).

17. **Can you provide references?** Talk to existing tenants of the landlord to get their feedback on their experience. They also can give you the insider's view on the local area and how the building operates, such as parking etiquette, mail services and pickup, and more.

Checklist: Finding Your Studio Space

☐ Make a list of requirements for expanding your current studio or moving to your next studio space.

☐ Research industrial and commercial properties in your area to understand the spaces available.

☐ Contact landlords and commercial real estate agents in your area to understand the timeline and next steps.

Next Up: How to Lay Out Your Studio Space
Use the most of your space by finding the best location for production, storage, walkways, and more.

CHAPTER 2 – HOW TO LAY OUT YOUR STUDIO SPACE

Considering basic areas needed for various tasks and uses, and how much space to allow for them. Determining how much space is needed for your studio and starting with a blank floor plan. Using paper or a computer to plan your studio layout.

You'll need:
-A list of activities performed in your studio.
-A tape measure for checking the measurements of your current space.
-A list of equipment, ingredients, and items stored in the studio.
-Paper and pen, a whiteboard, or a computer for listing items and sketching out your potential studio layout.

HOW MUCH SPACE DO YOU NEED?

Space Needs Vary, Even Between Similar Businesses
If you have many different products requiring different setups, ingredients, and packaging, you need more space. A limited number of products and product types require much less space. If you use your space well and manage inventories well (see Section 3), you can get away with a smaller and less expensive space. This chapter will help you to lay out your current studio and your next potential studio so you can use your current space better and have a firm idea of what to shop for when looking for new spaces.

Do You Find a New Space First, or Create a Layout?
Start by laying out your activities in your existing space, whether that's at home or in your current studio. This will tell you how much space you're currently using so you can set your requirements for minimum square footage during your property search. Use the same layout techniques to lay out potential new spaces when you are considering moving to a new location and have the dimensions of a prospective space.

Planning Extra Space for Growth
Cost is lowest when you find a space that suits your production needs today. But moving again in six months because you've outgrown your current space also is expensive. Consider how fast you plan to grow. The faster you are growing, the more extra space you will need. A good rule of thumb is to reserve at least 25-30% of a production space for future expansion.

YOUR LIST OF AREAS TO INCLUDE

To determine the size requirements of your studio, start by making a list of all the activities and storage requirements you currently have. Use this list as a guide for items to include. Also check for any local laws that apply to minimum workspaces, walkways, or other accessibility requirements in your area.

Walkways
You'll need to move both people and product around your studio. Smaller lanes work for people, and wider lanes are needed for equipment or bulk product. A width of 2.5 feet is enough space for a person to walk, and four to five feet is enough space to move a single standard pallet using a pallet jack. Create strips of area based on these widths and include them in your proposed layout to save this open area and segment your space for other activities.

Work Cells
In modern production, the most common, and typically the best way to lay out a station to perform work is a work cell shaped like an L or a U. This could be a single table with a standing area in front of it and ingredients on one side. The cell includes space for one or more people to work, surrounded by tables, equipment, and raw materials.

The standing area of the work cell should be enough room to move in—at least 2.5 feet of open space in front of the equipment or table. Planning for five-foot square work cells lined with tables (the standard depth of a table is 30 inches) for each major activity is a good start. If activities are already being done in your current space, measure the amount of space you are using now and use the actual dimensions.

Each process or activity on your list should be assigned to either a shared or dedicated area on your layout. Each studio will have different processes to consider, but some common activities include incoming inspection, product production, packing, shipping, cleanup, and equipment maintenance.

Figure 2-1. Typical size and layout of a work cell.

Ergonomics

When planning for each work area, keep in mind there is a limited comfortable range of movement. All the main activity should take place in this range of space, with any items outside of this space used infrequently or moved as needed.

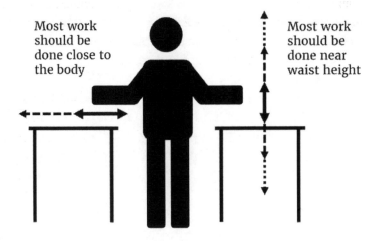

Figure 2-2. Ideal work zones.

Storage

Consider all raw materials, work-in-process (WIP), and finished product you intend to keep on hand. These items will be stored in areas such as pallets, cabinets, racks, and shelves. Designate an appropriate amount of storage based on your current product line, sales volume, and any new products you are planning for in the near future. If possible, install overhead racking or stacked storage racking. It's a good way to include storage and save space.

Equipment

Plan for space for your equipment items and enough room to comfortably and safely operate them. Equipment often needs to be located near an electrical or plumbing outlet, so make a note of any such requirements on your list of space needs.

Office and Meeting Area

Will you have non-production activities such as meetings and office work in this space? You may need desks, a coffee area, meeting spaces, a product display, a retail display area, restrooms, or a waiting area.

Assign Space for Each Activity

After you've compiled and checked your list of activities, use your current measurements, estimates, or the table below to assign an amount of space to each activity or storage need. When planning for equipment, look at available items on websites such as Global Industrial to get the dimensions. For layout purposes, some common dimensions are listed in Table 2-1.

Table 2-1. Typical Sizes for Various Activities and Items

Item	Description	Size
Aisle	For human walking	2.5 feet wide
Aisle	For forklifts (two passing)	12-20 feet
Aisle	For a single pallet	Four to five feet
Table	Typical depth	30 inches
Pallet	Standard size	40 x 48 inches
Work Cell	Work area—standing zone	Five square feet

List of Space Needs

After considering your own list of activities in your studio, compile a single list of all the activities that will take place in your factory, plus all product and equipment that will be present and an estimate of the necessary space for everything. Your list might look like the example in Table 2-2.

Table 2-2. Example List of Space Allocations

Area	Feature	Minimum	Expected
Storage	Raw materials: four pallets	50	75
	Finished goods: three racks + one pallet	100	100
	Soap curing racks	100	150
Office	Two desks	150	200
	Coffee and mini fridge	50	50
	Product display	50	50
Work Stations	Shipping	50	100
	Incoming inspection	Share with shipping	
	Soap-making (electric required)	150	200
	Cleanup—sink area (plumbing required)	50	50
	Subtotal	750	975
Other	Walkways: add ~25% to subtotal	188	250
	Room for growth: add ~25%+ to subtotal	188	500
	Total Square Footage	**1125**	**1725**

After you've allocated an amount of space to an activity or item, add up the total and include extra space for walkways and future growth plans. Does the overall estimate of your space needs match up with the dimensions of your current studio? You may discover extra space, or you may need to double up on some activities in a single work cell. Group work areas together if they will be used at the same time by the same person. This will cut down on moving product multiple times. After the list is complete, sketch out a floor plan and add in the working, moving, and storage requirements of your studio to create a proposed layout.

CREATING YOUR STUDIO LAYOUT

Obtain or Make a Sketch of the Floor Plan
All your activities must take place within the firm boundaries of your space: the walls, doors, windows, and so on. If possible, obtain a floor plan from your landlord. You also can sketch your own floor plan by taking measurements of the overall dimensions and the immovable parts (doors, windows, plumbing), and drawing them out on paper to be transferred to a poster, whiteboard, or computer. If you are starting from scratch to envision a future space, use a blank rectangle with approximate overall dimensions that are available in your area and within your budget. Your floor plan might look similar to the example in Figure 2-1. After you have a floor plan, add the working parts of your studio to see how everything will lay out.

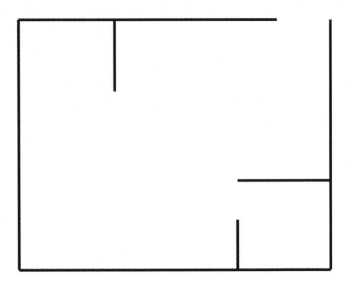

Figure 2-3. Floor Plan Created Using PowerPoint™

Poster Paper or Whiteboard
Having a to-scale diagram on the wall allows you to sketch out different options. Cut out sticky notes to represent areas and tables so you can move them around using rubber cement or magnet backing. Use a standard scale, such as 1:24 (one half inch on the model is one foot in real life), to keep things proportional.

Software-Based Layouts
Interior design software can be used to lay out your space. Use a simple drawing or sketching program to create the basic floor plan. After creating the floor plan on a computer, duplicate it and try new layouts. Again, use a standard scale to keep the model accurate.

Real-Life Rearranging
Physically rearrange your tables and equipment to try a new studio layout. Take photos of different arrangements to help decide which setup is best. This is the longest method and requires production to stop while you try new

layouts. Use this method on the best layout ideas you generate using other methods.

Use Your List to Add Areas to Your Layout

Do an imaginary walkthrough of your space and envision how various items will move. How will people get around? What's the path of your raw materials, WIP, and finished product? How do consumables and waste come in and out of the space? Your newly proposed layout might look similar to the example in Figure 2-4.

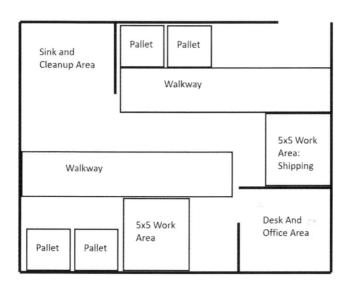

Figure 2-4. Same Space at Figure 2-3, Including Initial Layout

Spaghetti Diagrams

Using a copy of your current layout, trace the typical path you take when making a product or completing an order. Even better, physically complete a few tasks while someone else draws your movements on the diagram. This is called a spaghetti diagram because often it looks like you've drawn a mess of spaghetti. Seeing the lines from all your movement will show you what locations are out of place and give you ideas for how to reassemble your layout to minimize the amount of time and movement for your common activities.

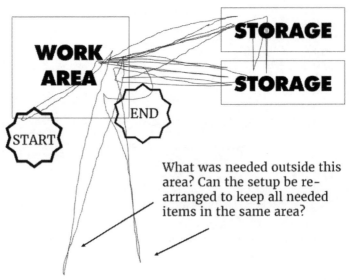

Figure 2-5. Spaghetti Diagram of Filling a Customer Order

Checklist: Laying Out Your Studio Space

☐ Create a list of areas that need to fit into your layout and determine how much space is needed for them.

☐ Obtain or create a floor plan of the overall dimensions and important immovable features in your space.

☐ Use paper, a whiteboard, or a computer to put each working and storage area into your overall layout.

☐ Move items in real space to create your working studio.

☐ Make changes as needed on your layout and in real life using the spaghetti diagram technique.

Next Up: Section Two
Keep your studio clean and orderly.

SECTION TWO: ORGANIZING YOUR STUDIO

CHAPTER 3 – INTRODUCTION TO 5S

An organized factory is safer, results in fewer mistakes, and produces superior products. Getting and staying organized is a continuous cycle through sort, set in order, shine, standardize, and sustain.

WHY START WITH 5S?

Start With The Obvious

In the world of manufacturing secrets, "keep your studio clean" seems a little too obvious. It's tempting to want to start with something more novel, like a new inventory management system or buying new equipment, and figure out the whole cleanliness thing later. However, organizing your existing space is foundational and will give a solid place to work from when adding new systems.

Before you create and stick to new and complicated procedures, your space should be clean, and you and staff should have the discipline to follow cleaning and organizing procedures. After all, if you can't set and follow procedures to keep your space clean, how can you set and follow more complicated procedures? You want to eventually have standards and procedures to adhere to safety standards, good manufacturing practice, product creation specifications, and perhaps even an externally audited standard such as organic certification. The basic hygiene discipline needed and practiced in the 5S method prepares you and your space for implementing these standards.

Dirty or Clean, Which is Better?

If you walk into a restaurant and the bathroom is filthy, do you feel differently about eating there? It's often said that the state of the bathroom indicates the quality of the food. A dirty bathroom indicates poor management and a staff that isn't proud of its place of work. A dirty workspace shows your clients and yourself that hygiene doesn't matter. How does that reflect on the quality of your products?

Two Studios—Which One Is Where You Want to Work?

Studio One

Imagine you are about to stop working for the day when you see a sale come through on your website. You've got an order to get out, hooray! You go to pack it up, only to find there is something on the shipping counter—labels that were delivered earlier, which you haven't yet put away. You take the arriving materials to the storage area and leave them in the box—you'll have to deal with it later. You return to the shipping counter to pack the items and realize you are out of stock on one ordered item. You'll need to make this product before you ship the order. You begin making the product. Phew, it looks like you got lucky—the labels that just arrived will be used here! You don't have time to organize them so you pull out a single label and leave the rest in the original box to deal with later. Your alarm goes off—it's time to run a personal errand. You still haven't shipped out the order so you leave the packing material from the open box on the floor as you dash out the door.

Studio Two

You get an alert that you received an order. You've got 10 minutes before you need to leave the shop—good thing that's plenty of time to get this done. You walk to the shipping table, which is clear of clutter, and quickly pack up the order because everything you need is at hand and ready to be used. You leave five minutes ahead of schedule, which gives you enough time to swing by the post office. Your customer is surprised and delighted to get a shipping notification so quickly after placing an order and is even happier when the item arrives a few days later.

A Clean Studio Makes Better Product

With your clean and organized shop, you can adapt quickly to customer needs and orders. Products have fewer defects, lower costs, fewer delays, and fewer customer complaints. Except for rare cases, you have no injuries, no equipment breakdowns, and no mixed-up orders. You can focus on the growth of your business instead of spending time frustrated and looking for

... You feel calmer with a safer, cleaner space where clients can drop by and are impressed with your gleaming studio.

A Tried and True Method

To move your shop from messy, disorganized, and hard to work to clean and streamlined, there is no need to invent a new system. Large manufacturing companies around the world have been following a well-established formal process originally developed in Japan known as 5S for decades. It consists of five steps, repeated, as needed, through a cycle to continually make the workplace cleaner and better. The five original terms in Japanese are in the table below, followed by the rough translation now used to represent the terms in English.

Table 3-1. Common Translation of Japanese 5S Terms

Japanese Term	English Version
Seiri 整理	Sort
Seiton 整頓	Set in order
Seisō 清掃	Shine
Seiketsu 清潔	Standardize
Shitsuke 躾	Sustain

Sort

Get rid of anything that doesn't belong in the work area where you are standing. This does not necessarily mean an item is thrown away permanently, but that it is removed from the immediate area. If it isn't needed at the station, it must go somewhere else.

Set in Order

Arrange the needed items in a way that makes them easy to find, use, and put away. You may think of the phrase "a place for everything, and everything in its place." Each item will have a home and you'll know at a glance where it belongs and whether something is missing.

Shine
Your factory and equipment is clean: free of dust, dirt, pests, and contaminants.

Standardize
Adopt habits and methods to make sure the first three activities are not a one-time event. This includes a regular cleaning schedule and times for washing items and returning them to their homes.

Sustain
After you have established homes for items and a plan for keeping everything in order, execute the plan for the long term. Habits take a long time to form; don't let the initial energy burst of having a clean factory fade away and your workshop return to the old, disorganized way.

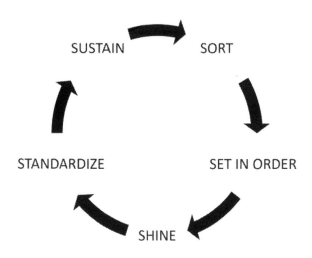

Figure 3-1. 5S Components Represented as a Continuous Cycle

COMMON PROBLEMS

These are some common feelings of resistance to adopting 5S:

1. I already know where everything is! As long as no one else needs to ever find things, I don't need to reorganize.
2. I'm too busy to label and sort everything all the time.
3. Why clean? It will just get dirty again.
4. I'm an expert at making products, not cleaning.
5. I already tried being organized. I work better as a tortured, sloppy genius.
6. Things are fine. I don't need to improve.

Overcoming Resistance to a Clean Studio

Many makers skip organization to work on product fulfillment and other topics. It's common to feel frustrated and express something like one of the above statements. But implementing other tools won't work without the discipline of putting something back in its place and keeping it clean.

If you have or intend to hire employees, their ability to follow the basic hygiene rules of the workplace during training will be a great indication of whether they will bring discipline to the more complicated procedures in your factory. Every other manufacturing system—from inventory management to automated equipment operation—is built on the fundamentals of following directions and keeping things in the right place. These skills are critical and provide a strong base upon which to build your factory operations.

```
┌─────────────────────────────────────────────────┐
│          Checklist: Preparing for 5S             │
│                                                   │
│   ☐  Set aside a full day or half day to complete │
│      the first step, Chapter 4 – Sort.            │
│                                                   │
│                                                   │
└─────────────────────────────────────────────────┘
```

Next Up: Sort

You have an idea what to expect from the five steps. Next, implement sort to get unneeded items out of your way.

CHAPTER 4 – SORT

Sorting means getting items out of your way. The result is workstations that include the required items and nothing else.

You'll need:
-A half-day to full day set aside to complete all of your sorting at once.
-A camera for before and after photos.
-A bin, red tags, and an area set aside as your "red-tag" area.
-Sticky notes or other method of labelling items.

WHY SORT?

Workstations Often Feel Crowded

When there are many items nearby, we convince ourselves we need "more space" to operate. Often, a small space is enough if it's used well. By removing unneeded items, it's clear whether the workstation is big enough to perform the task. By sorting out the needed items from everything else, you can make the most of the space you have and prepare for further organizing.

HOW TO SORT USING RED TAGS

Find and Move Everything That's Not Needed in the Immediate Area

Everything in the studio will be checked and all items will be left only if they are of use. Block off enough time to go through the entire studio in a single effort—typically a few hours to a full day. First, take a "before" photo of the studio. You'll be able to reflect on the stages of this process and see great progress in a short amount of time. Determine what items are unnecessary and need to be removed from the work area. To avoid convincing yourself an item is definitely needed at some point in the future, choose a time frame. A common time frame is one month—decide whether the item is needed in the area in the next month. Every single object in your workspace will fall into one of two (and only two) categories.

Is this item needed in this area (in the next month)?

1. If YES, keep it. This item now lives in this area and you'll keep it there and do more with it in Step S2 (set in order).
2. If NO, it goes to the red-tag area.

Identify Items Out of Place With Red Tags

Red tagging is the term and system used by lean manufacturing teams at big factories when labeling an item for evaluation and potential disposal. This is because the color red is used to mark off an area and red is used to color the physical tags placed on items. The red color makes it clear which items are out of place, and makes it easier to flag a large piece of equipment rather than moving it right away. You also can use colored sticky notes, colored tape or string tied to items. The main objective is to make it very clear which items are needed and which are not. For portable items and equipment, it's most effective simply to remove them from the workspace and place them in a holding area. Additionally, red tags can be used to identify the name or use of an item if it's not clear from looking at it.

Sort Quickly
Don't waste time trying to determine the future destination of an item during the sorting stage. If it's not needed in the work area, it gets red-tagged. Only obvious garbage (such as empty boxes or broken tools) can be disposed of. Everything else goes to the red-tag area.

If it Gets Used, it Can Stay
You don't need to change your approach or try to be a minimalist to accomplish sorting. For example, if you regularly use five different scrapers at a station, that's OK. They can all stay. You simply are getting rid of any items that are unneeded and not used at this station. After your area is clear, you may realize the only reason you needed five scrapers was because you couldn't find one when you needed it.

Examples of Things to Red Tag
Red-tag product that's partially made (Work-In-Process, or WIP, inventory), research projects, raw materials not used in the area, finished products, obsolete equipment, tools that are used in a different area, broken parts, extra office supplies, worktables not being used, and anything you are unsure of.

Examples of Things to Keep
Keep tools and equipment used for the process at hand. Keep cleanup materials, such as rags, if they are used in this area. Also keep items like tables, safety equipment, and floor mats.

✓ Clean out drawers again. Reduce items in the drawers
✓ Throw out old botanicals

valuable

...y useful things stay in your work area. Everything else, including valuable items or items you might sell, give away, or use for a future purpose, go to the red-tag area. Think of the red-tag area as a holding zone for any item that doesn't have a clear, immediate purpose.

DEALING WITH THE RED-TAG AREA

After the entire area has been sorted, turn your attention to the red-tag items. It's possible you won't look at these items the same day as you place them in the area—that's OK. The goal is to get everything that isn't immediately needed into one place. As you use your workstations, you may need to come to the red-tag area to recover an item caught in the wrong place during the sort.

When You're Ready to Address the Red-Tag Items
Determine if the item is needed in the studio. If it is, it will get assigned a home during the next chapter, Set In Order. If it's not needed anywhere in your studio for the next month, either store it in an organized way, recycle, donate, or throw it out.

Storing Items Needed Long Term
For product samples, seasonally used items, and project work you want to retain, label a box with clear project information. Place related items into the box and store it in a long-term storage area or offsite. A clearly labeled box will help you find the item if it's needed, or help clean out unneeded items from storage.

Get Rid of Items Without an Immediate or Future Use
Sell the item to another company or person who can use it. Donate it to a local organization, such as an art supplier, teacher's swap circle, or tool lending library. Recycle or landfill the item. If it's not useful to you or someone else, it's time to let go.

Getting Rid of Items Often Is the Most Difficult Step

Don't let this step get in the way of your improvements! Make sure your red-tag area is out of the way of your studio activities, get rid of items as an ongoing activity when you have time. The great news is these maybe-needed items are no longer hanging around, unused, in the work area, and the main studio can be organized.

Take an 'After' Photo of Your Studio

A common outcome of a successful sort is you feel like you can breathe easier with all the extra room in your area. You've made room for valuable equipment and materials, and have the space to make better product. You'll use this space well in the next step.

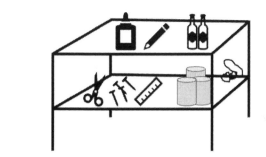

Figure 4-1. Before Sorting

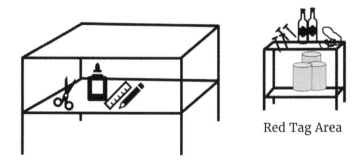

Red Tag Area

Figure 4-2. Sort: Items Removed And Placed in Separate Red-Tag Area

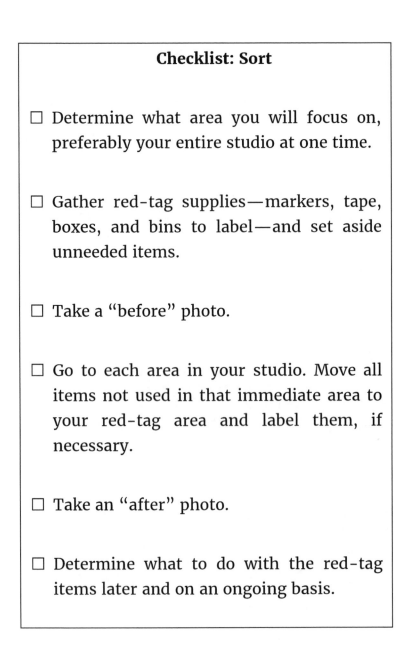

Checklist: Sort

☐ Determine what area you will focus on, preferably your entire studio at one time.

☐ Gather red-tag supplies—markers, tape, boxes, and bins to label—and set aside unneeded items.

☐ Take a "before" photo.

☐ Go to each area in your studio. Move all items not used in that immediate area to your red-tag area and label them, if necessary.

☐ Take an "after" photo.

☐ Determine what to do with the red-tag items later and on an ongoing basis.

Next Up: Set in Order

Now that you have only what you need in your workplace, it's time to get your markers and labels out, and assign homes to all those useful things!

CHAPTER 5 – SET IN ORDER

Find a designated home for each item that remains in the workspace. Each item becomes easier to find and put away.

You'll need:
-Colored tape.
-Markers.
-String.
-Storage bins.
-Label maker or permanent marker.

WHY SET IN ORDER?

Why Label Everything When You're the Only One Working?
Even if you're the only one who needs to know where things are, you still should set up your factory so you can run it when you are tired at the end of the day. After making every decision for your business and studio, having items set in order is a kindness that helps you avoid mistakes.

It also prepares for temporary or permanent employees to enter the workplace and do the processes you do. Without an orderly shop, new employees are left to guess what belongs where. It's a gift to give someone a job *and* the tools needed to be confident they are doing it right. Do that for yourself, as well as current and future employees.

HOW TO SET IN ORDER

Start With Only What's Needed
After getting rid of unneeded items (sort), confirm you have all the needed items in your workspace. For example, a tool for opening bucket lids may have been in the wrong location during sort and placed in the red-tag area. You may want to work for a few days in the new space and allow materials to come to their homes. You'll also notice there are some shared tools— perhaps a pair of scissors is used both at a manufacturing station to open bags and at the shipping station to cut paper. Whenever possible, all items should stay at the correct station so they are available when needed. Buy another pair of scissors.

 Arrange Items in Order of Use Frequency
Just like the home row keys on a keyboard, the tools and supplies you use most frequently should be the easiest to reach. Prioritize these items and

then use the methods in this chapter to identify the items and their proper place.

There Are Many Different Methods Used to Implement Set in Order
The rest of this chapter outlines different ways to organize and label items, with examples. You can combine them as well.

A Few Ways to Set in Order

1. Physically bolt or tether items in the place they are used.
2. Place sets of tools for different activities in separate kits.
3. Hang pegboards to display items and tools in the work area.
4. Color code items that are used together.
5. Name storage locations for items/inventory and create a whiteboard address book to show storage locations.
6. Paint/outline item locations on a board, table, bin, or the floor.
7. Create a checklist of needed items for a task.

Physically Bolt or Tether Items in the Place They Are Used

Real-life example: A pen physically attached to a string on a clipboard or credit card station.

Studio example: A shipping station with shipping supplies tied to keep them in one location.

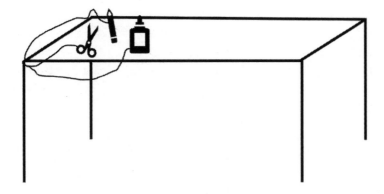

Figure 5-1. Tethered Items in Place

Place Sets of Tools for Different Activities in Separate Kits

Create kits of tools, parts, or ingredients for different activities. Create different kits for different product development projects, private label clients or other projects. Each can be put away and worked on separately.

Real-life example: Puzzles. Each set of pieces is kept in their own box, and all the boxes are stored in one work (play) station. If you're going to assemble a puzzle, you don't dump out all the pieces you own—you start with the set of pieces from the puzzle you want to assemble.

Shop example: A single set of tools all used for one purpose. When opening a drum of oil, four different hand tools are used: a scraper to cut through the foil cap, pliers to remove the foil, a bung opener to open the drum, and screwdrivers to move the wrap heater from the old drum to the newly opened one. Rather than collect this set of tools from the maintenance area each time you need them, or leave them in a pile near the drums, they stay in a labeled kit.

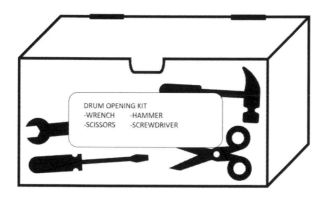

Figure 5-2. Kits Keep Items Together

Hang Pegboards to Display Items and Tools in the Work Area

Real-life example: Gardening and yard tools hanging on a pegboard in the garage.

Shop example: Tools on a pegboard.

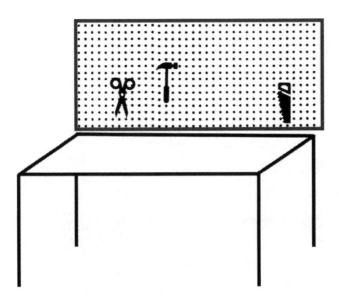

Figure 5-3. Pegboard holding tools in place

Should I tape where seasonal fragrances go? tape where "BB stuff" goes?

Color Code Items That Are Used Together

Use colored markers and tape to indicate the storage location for different items, especially in sets. Perhaps all materials for one product line are blue. Place colored tape on the bins and floor storage location to show where they belong. This makes it immediately clear when something is out of place or missing, and the location to where it should be returned.

Real–life example: Maps for public transit systems and train lines. Seeing colors on a map, especially for multilingual cities with range of literacy, helps provide easier navigation.

Shop example: Labeling essential oils to make the bottles easier to distinguish.

Figure 5–4. Color Coded Items

Name Storage Locations for Items/Inventory and Create a Whiteboard Address Book to Show Storage Locations

This works well for big locations or when you're moving between a work area and a storage location in the basement or garage. This also works well for inventory storage of raw materials, WIP, and finished goods. Name the storage areas after their use, such as "raw materials storage" or alphanumeric codes, such as "Shelf A5." Then create a board showing the location of items.

Real-life example: Supermarket aisles. Looking for pasta? It's in aisle three. Jam? Aisle five. Like an old-fashioned address book, you can look up the name of your friend to find out where they live.

Shop example: Create, name, and label storage locations with numbers, letters, or names. "It's in the back" is less clear than "It's on shelf four" or "It's in the label cabinet."

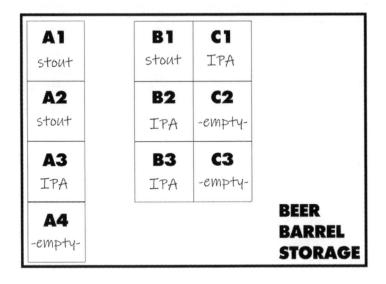

Figure 5-5. Storage Locations on a Whiteboard Map

Paint/Outline Item Locations on a Board, Table, Bin, or the Floor

Real-life example: Parking spots and lines. When parking, each car uses a slot that's bounded by lines and sometimes numbered by spot, floor, or area.

Shop example: Pallet storage and equipment home areas are outlined and labeled on the floor so items can be returned to the correct place.

Figure 5-6. Storage Locations, Outlined and Labeled

Create a Checklist of Needed Items for a Task

Ideally, any checklist of items also has the items close at hand, but for small studios you may be sharing equipment between multiple stations and activities. If buying multiple tools to keep a set at each location is not yet realistic, this checklist method allows you to use what you already have in the studio. Make a checklist of what tools are needed for each job. Rather than moving locations to perform the new job, pull out the checklist before starting the job and make sure everything is present, obtaining tools from other stations or a central location.

Real-life example: Furniture assembly instructions with a photo list of the parts and tools needed to assemble the item.

Shop example: Checklist of items needed for a sales show. Because sellable product is unlikely to be stored in the same location as your canopy tent, a checklist provides a reliable way to ensure you have everything you need, and it gives you nearly the same ease as keeping everything together.

Figure 5-7. Checklist of Needed Items for Event

Checklist: Set In Order

☐ Take a "before" photo.

☐ Ensure sort is complete and you have only the needed items in your area.

☐ Find a place for everything. Arrange items in the space, considering frequency of use.

☐ Put everything in place. Tether, label, outline, and color code items into their new homes.

☐ Take a step back and make sure places are still clear. Add signage or color, if needed.

☐ Take an "after" photo.

Next Up: Shine

Now that all your items are easy to access and where they should be, it's time to make your workshop shine. In the next chapter, you'll learn why keeping a clean space is so important to your business, and how to get it done.

CHAPTER 6 – SHINE

A clean studio is both style and substance.

You'll need:
-Rags or paper towels.
-Cleaning and sanitizing materials.
-Water.
-Brooms, mops, buckets, and trash cans.

WHY SHINE?

Clean and Organized Go Together

During sort and set in order, you probably came across the grime and grit attached to little-used items. You probably cleaned up and wiped down areas before setting items back—that's natural to do when preparing to use any item. Keeping equipment clean and ready to use on a constant basis includes all the previous steps: no extra items in your work area, everything ready at hand where it's needed, and all equipment clean. Imagine yourself as a fussy restaurant chef, insisting on having all tools at hand and a spotless kitchen. Refusing to work in a dirty kitchen is a reasonable choice for a professional chef—would they want to work in your studio?

A common mistake is to think regular cleaning is a surface-level activity that's not really needed for real factory work. But a clean shop gives you two things.

1. **Style.** An atmosphere of discipline and cleanliness, where you're proud to work and comfortable inviting in a potential client who drops by.
2. **Substance.** A safe, highly functional studio that's ready at a moment's notice to spring into action to make product without worry of contamination.

Dirty equipment hides problems like leaks, frayed wires, and worn parts. Cleaning equipment regularly prevents these problems from interrupting your business by allowing time to inspect and identify issues.

Here are some examples of how shine works in your favor:

- A cutting blade with a chip is found during cleaning. Knowing the material is washed after each batch, the chip can be found in the last batch of production and avoids a major potential safety issue.

- The plastic bowl in a mixer is gradually wearing out. During a cleaning step one day, you notice the bottom is nearly worn through.

You replace the bowl before any breakage occurs, and there is no disruption to production.

HOW TO SHINE

Clean Everything
During the shine step of your 5S, give every piece of equipment a thorough wash or wipe down. Soap, water, rags, and elbow grease are the main tools to be used.

Maintain Equipment
Check the maintenance guides of any equipment for recommended maintenance steps. Clean and lubricate moving parts. Replace batteries, and check wires and electrical connections for fraying. Inspect paint and other coatings for signs of wear. Calibrate scales and other measuring equipment.

These cleaning activities should become automatic and part of the tasks performed in making all your products. They will be standardized and sustained during the following chapters.

What's Broken or Could Be Better?
While cleaning, keep a maintenance to-do list ready. Keep track of equipment that should be replaced, major repairs to be done, and replacement parts that need to be ordered.

SHOULD YOU OUTSOURCE CLEANING?

Cleaning Is Time Consuming and Usually Not the Fun Part of Making Product

It's tempting to hire a cleaning service or have a single employee to "deal with" the initial and ongoing task of keeping items and the space clean. However, because of the importance of fully inspecting equipment during cleaning, it should not be outsourced. The person who uses the equipment should keep it clean. They will notice when something is wrong and not just wipe it down and move on.

The ownership of keeping a space clean belongs to those who work there; you and your workers should not take the attitude that you're there to work and it's someone else's job to clean up.

Checklist: Shine

☐ Take a "before" photo.

☐ Wash or wipe down all items.

☐ Perform maintenance on equipment: check for leaks, fraying, chipping, wear, and contamination. Calibrate equipment, replace batteries, lubricate, and tighten loose parts.

☐ Wipe down walls, ceiling fixtures, doors, and other areas not actively used.

☐ Sweep and mop the floor.

☐ Remove trash and recycling.

☐ Take an "after" photo.

Next Up: Standardize.
Your studio is clean and orderly. Next, make a plan to keep it that way.

CHAPTER 7 – STANDARDIZE

Standardizing is finding ways to repeat the first steps on a regular basis by folding them into regular factory operations so equipment and workstations are always clean and ready to be used.

You'll need:
-A list of your standard operating procedures.
-Access to your calendar or scheduling system.

WHY STANDARDIZE?

Keep it Going!

You've powered through to sort, set in order, and shine. Your studio looks amazing and the best it's ever been—and then the clock starts ticking. How long until things slip back to their old ways? Standardize will help you formalize cleaning and organization and make sure it is really part of what you do every day. In other words, you've already done everything to keep things in order, now the hard part of forming good habits begins!

Organizing the studio should not be reinvented each time one item is out of place. This would be like coming up with a new recipe for lip balm each time you make it. Your company doesn't have time for that kind of ill-directed effort. You want a standard recipe that is done the same way, every time. It's the same with cleaning up and keeping organized.

In addition, regular cleaning is a requirement of many systems including good manufacturing practice (GMP). Cleaning all parts of the equipment, floor, and product contact surfaces helps prevent contamination and pest issues. A clean area contributes to a more streamlined operation because production work can start as soon as you arrive in the shop rather than delaying production by requiring cleanup before there is enough room to move. A clean shop also is ready at any time for an unexpected drop in from an important client or inspectors from local government offices such as the U.S. Food and Drug Administration.

HOW TO STANDARDIZE

To keep things clean, they should start clean and then stay that way. Consider the different ways materials and equipment get dirty in your space. Clean things when they get to your space, as they are used, and regularly.

Incoming Inspection and Cleaning

Clean any raw materials as they enter your space. Many shipments have dust or grime from storage and transport.

Any Standard Operating Procedures, Whether Written or Unwritten, Should Include Cleanup

Different activities may require different types of cleanup—from washing the equipment to sweeping the floor. If you have a written procedure for a job, always include the required cleanup steps. If you don't have written procedures, this is a good time to start! Start with a checklist for cleaning up an area and add in production activities to your procedure later. The main point is to get in the habit of never leaving an area to start a new job until things are cleaned up. Do you need to check inventory levels and restock items? This is the perfect end-of-shift activity to add to cleanup.

Table 7-1. Example of a Daily Checklist for Filling Station

Production	• Check production area for empty bins.
	• Make product to fill all empty bins.
Inventory	• Enter daily production into inventory sheet.
	• Refill bottle caps from storage bin.
Cleanup	• Turn off scale and wipe down.
	• Wipe down countertop.

Scheduled Cleaning

Along with the cleaning that occurs as part of regular activities, some cleaning can go on the calendar to ensure it gets done on a regular schedule. Daily, weekly, monthly, and yearly cleaning can be scheduled to ensure things are kept in good shape.

Table 7-2. Example of a Cleaning Schedule

As Used	• Wash equipment, wipe down countertops, sweep floor area • wipe down incoming materials.
Daily	• Put away washed items that have dried overnight. • Work on any irregular cleaning tasks not tied to a particular work area. • Clean up full-day work areas such as desks.
Weekly	• Sweep and mop the floor. • Walk through facility and check for items needing straightening or labeling.
Monthly	• Wipe down and clean out storage areas.
Annually	• Wipe down walls, ceiling fixtures, and other areas not actively involved in production. • Check for maintenance issues on window screens, doors and facilities.

The Five-Minute 5S Walk

Designate five minutes regularly to walk the floor with only the 5S steps in mind. Keep a sharp eye for items in the wrong place, anything out of order, and dirty areas. First thing in the morning, after lunch, or before leaving for the day are good times for this walk.

Never, Ever, Walk Past a Piece of Trash on the Floor

Picking up stray packing peanuts and bits of cardboard not only helps solidify the habit of keeping things in order, it keeps the plant safer by reducing potential trips and slips.

Checklist: Standardize

☐ Develop and write out standard cleanup activities that will go with each standard operating procedure in your studio.

☐ Create a standard cleanup plan that includes daily, weekly, monthly, and annual cleanup activities and put these on your calendar.

☐ Designate a time for your five-minute 5S walk each day.

Next Up: Sustain.
You've standardized your 5S activities and you're getting in the habit of keeping things in order. Sustain will guide you through making organization part of your key operations for the long term.

CHAPTER 8 – SUSTAIN

Sustain means making a commitment to monitoring the organization of the studio as part of managing the overall business.

You'll need:
-Accountability partners.
-Reference books and other sources for improvement ideas.
-Whiteboard or other location to keep a running list of improvement ideas.

WHY SUSTAIN?

Keep it Going ... Again
Be honest—did you hope going through the activities in this section would be a one-time thing, and that after reading it and putting in some hours you'd have an organized factory for the rest of time? If only that could be the case.

The first few steps can be done with willpower. But to keep your studio improving, you need to make organizing a habit.

HOW TO SUSTAIN

Make It a Habit
During standardize, we talked about adding cleaning steps along with regular daily activities such as production. Studies from Stanford's Behavior Design Lab show that habits are easier to form when they are linked to tasks that are already a habit. So, if you're trying to increase the behavior of cleaning up, make sure you always clean up at the same time or after the same triggering event, such as finishing the batch or just after recording the batch information.

In the same way, almost any trick you use for other habits may help with the larger goal of getting your studio in order. Here are some tried and true tricks for sticking with a new habit:

Form an Accountability Group
Form a group or partnership with another studio owner and do a walkthrough of each other's spaces once per month rather than meeting at a coffee shop to discuss business ideas.

Introduce the Carrot and Stick Approach
Create treats for yourself when your factory meets your expectations a certain number of days in a row, or purchase your competitor's product if things are not up to par.

Publicly Declare Your Commitments
Post on social media that you're working on a project for your factory and commit to posting one photo per week of your transformation.

As the organized factory becomes more of a habit, you'll not only sustain the improvements you've made but also be able to add more. If you've started using labeling and color-coding, expand on this by noticing and adding more labels and color to the workplace. Add additional signage to areas or replace small labels with bigger, easier to read signs. Refer to this book or one of the reference materials at the end of the chapter to choose next steps to continue to improve.

Here are some ways to keep improving each of the 5S steps after your initial efforts:

Next Steps for Sort
Use only the space necessary for each job. Tables and storage areas that are bigger than needed tend to collect unnecessary items.

Next Steps for Set in Order
Reduce the number of tools needed for a job by modifying the steps needed. Use wall and cabinet storage rather than tabletop storage so it's clear at a glance that the factory is in order when all the tables are clear and clean. Make signs and labels larger so they can be read clearly from further away.

Next Steps for Shine
What's better than cleaning things regularly? Keeping them from getting dirty in the first place. Make changes to processes so they are less messy to begin with, such as spill guards on ingredient storage containers. Use tables with a backsplash so you don't have materials falling between the table and

wall. Install covers and overhangs to keep debris out of products. Use a floor mat at your entrance. Place screens on the windows. Wipe down these items regularly.

Next Steps for Standardize

What checklist steps are useful? Can you move from written procedures to photos or pictograms to show steps at a quick glance in written procedures? Is there a better time of the week for deep cleaning than you have now? Reevaluate your regular cleaning schedule and find ways to match it to the rhythm of your factory. If large orders go out on Tuesdays, then Wednesdays are a good day for mopping the floor.

Next Steps for Sustain

Keep making improvements. A separate to-improve list helps keep improvement ideas safe until they are ready to implement, and distinguishes them from regular production tasks. A whiteboard or corner of one can contain upcoming improvement projects.

BENCHMARKING FOR IMPROVEMENTS

Ideas Come From Everywhere

It's difficult to continue coming up with fresh ways to improve the organization at your own factory, especially if you're the only one working there. A great way to keep improving is by benchmarking your production efforts with other companies. Find local companies, like breweries, that offer tours of production. Seeing other products being made can be helpful whether the products you manufacture are similar or very different.

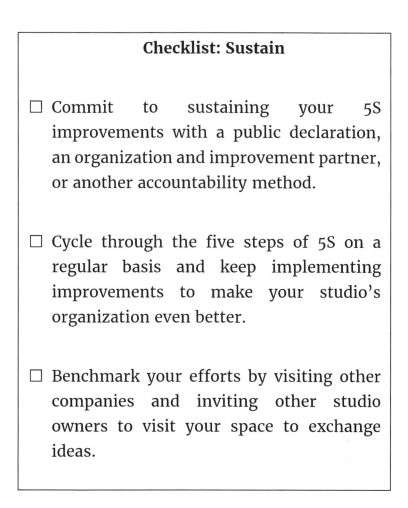

Checklist: Sustain

☐ Commit to sustaining your 5S improvements with a public declaration, an organization and improvement partner, or another accountability method.

☐ Cycle through the five steps of 5S on a regular basis and keep implementing improvements to make your studio's organization even better.

☐ Benchmark your efforts by visiting other companies and inviting other studio owners to visit your space to exchange ideas.

Next Up: Section Three
Running your studio, from filling orders to re-ordering materials.

SECTION THREE:
RUNNING YOUR STUDIO

CHAPTER 9 – PULL SYSTEMS IN THE STUDIO

How a pull system differs from a push system, and why you should set up pull whenever possible.

You'll need:
-One cooked spaghetti noodle or other string-like item.

Pulling the Noodle

Spaghetti noodles are like production systems: they seem pretty simple until you try to move one where you want it to go. Try pushing on one end of a cooked noodle on a countertop. It bunches up into a tangled mess. Now try gently pulling on the end of the noodle. It follows your hand in a neat line. Rugs, beach towels, toy trains, noodles—these are all physical examples that remind us that pulling on something is the best way to keep it orderly while moving. So, what does a pull system look like in your studio?

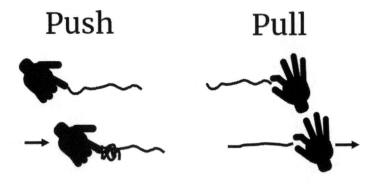

Figure 9-1. Pushing and Pulling a Noodle

PRODUCT FLOW

Figure 9-2. Activities to Get Raw Materials Through the Studio

How Product Moves Through the Studio

Think about a single item moving through your studio. The journey from your suppliers to your customers is listed below, broken out by chapter.

- Chapter 13: Purchasing and Supply Chain (Buy). You find and buy raw materials. They are purchased and received at your studio.
- Chapter 12: Inventory Management (Hold). You store the materials until they are ready to be used in production.
- Chapter 11: Production Scheduling (Make). You turn the raw materials into finished products ready for sale.
- Chapter 10: Filling Orders (Ship). You sell the products and deliver to your customer.

You may notice the order of materials moving through your studio is opposite to the order covered in this book. When using a Pull system, we start at the end, with customer orders. All other activities take place to support sales. We will start with filling orders in Chapter 10 and then work all the way back to buying materials.

Pulling Product

Starting with a customer order is like pulling on the noodle. Start with the sales order and then move along the rest of the process to follow the order and keep the noodle straight. Starting with the sales order allows all activities in the studio to be based on actual demand, not forecasts. It lets you make product only if there is a need for it, so less time and materials are wasted. Pulling materials through your production system keeps everything neat and efficient.

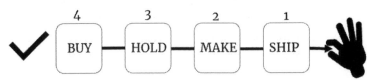

Figure 9-3 Pulling Product Through the Studio

Pushing Product

If you instead run your system according to forecasts—pushing on the noodle—you keep piling in raw material and storing it, making product without waiting for actual demand, and storing it even if no one is buying it. You run out of some products because they are more popular than you expected and you haven't scheduled time to make them. You keep making product because of the forecasted schedule, not because of what your customers are actually buying. Pushing on your production system should be avoided whenever possible.

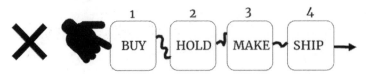

Figure 9-4 Pushing Product Through the Studio

PULL SYSTEMS AT THE STORE AND STUDIO

Restocking a Grocery Store

Your local grocery store carries shelves full of items ready to be purchased as soon as you walk in the door. Shelves are restocked according to what gets sold, with the goal of always keeping a few items on the shelf. If there is too much inventory, the store needs a huge space and risks products expiring before they sell. Too little inventory and the items will sell out, leaving an empty store where no one wants to shop. By stocking a small inventory and replacing items according to sales, the store stays in business.

Your studio should take the same approach. Product should be made only to the demand of the customers purchasing products. Raw materials should be ordered to meet the demand of the production process, which meets the demand of the customer. All the activities in the studio set their pace with customer orders.

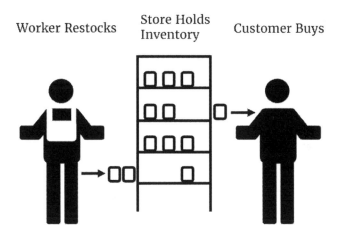

Worker Restocks   Store Holds Inventory   Customer Buys

Figure 9-5. Grocery Store Restocking To Match Customer Orders

Stores Hold Items Until They're Needed

Anywhere inventory is stored in your studio can be referred to as a store. When filling an order, you get finished products from your finished products store. When doing production, you get your ingredients from your raw materials store. Each of the various storage areas is run in a similar way to a grocery store, being replenished according to demand.

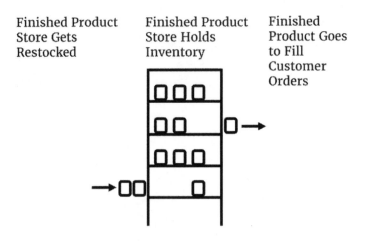

Figure 9-6. Studio Store Restocking to Match Customer Orders

An Order Pulls the Product Flow Through Your Studio

A customer places an order and is sent product as soon as possible—usually from stocked inventory (your finished products store) or items that are quickly custom-built from waiting WIP. The customer is happy. The factory now has work to do to move the rest of the product forward to be ready for the next order. Additional finished product is made to replenish the store shelves. Any additional WIP is made to replenish the WIP store. Orders are placed to replenish the raw material store.

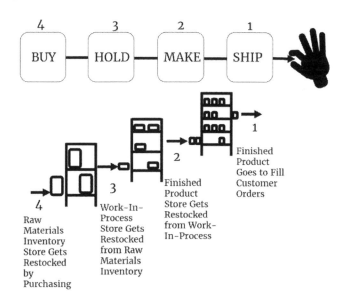

Figure 9-7. Restocking Multiple Stores As Items Are Sold

PULL VS. PUSH SYSTEMS

The main differences between a pull system and a push system are summarized In Table 9-1.

Table 9-1. Pull Systems vs. Push Systems

Pull Systems	Push Systems
✓ Pulling a noodle in a straight line.	✗ Bunching up the noodle by pushing it.
✓ Use actual demand to purchase and produce product.	✗ Base all activities on expected demand.
✓ Make product that's being sold.	✗ Guess at what product will sell.
✓ Respond to today's customer needs quickly.	✗ Work from customer requests from the past.
✓ Flexible to meet changes in demand.	✗ Static, work to expected demand.
✓ Use studio time efficiently, making product customers want.	✗ Work to the schedule, actual sales orders be darned.
✓ Inventory levels stay low.	✗ High inventory levels needed to cover all possible demand for orders.

Pulling: Let Your Sales Make Your Decisions for You

Autopilot is a crucial part of flying a plane. It is used to save attention and energy for the part of the flight where the pilot's skills and decisions are needed. Wasting that energy during the easily auto-piloted segment of the flight means you have a tired pilot who needs to make decisions the entire time.

Think of using a studio pull system like autopilot: You want to have the autopilot on as much as possible so you can save your attention for items that require it. For parts of your production that are easy to put on autopilot, why use your valuable time and skills to manage them? Default to using a pull system when you can; use push when you must. Here are some examples of situations where each type of system makes sense.

Existing Product Line: Pull
Whenever demand is somewhat steady for a product over time, use a pull system to make the product and replenish raw materials.

Custom Orders: Pull
By definition, custom orders are made in response to an order for a customer.

Fast-Growing Business: Pull
When there is an increasing amount of demand for your product, it's important to reevaluate how much you keep in the store. Instead of a small number of items replaced weekly, you may need to keep more items in the store or replace them daily to keep up with demand. Either way, you still can act in response to customer demand. How much is in the store (inventory management) and how you replenish it (production scheduling) is discussed further in Chapters 11 and 12.

New Product Launch: Push
For new products, you don't have any sales yet, so there's no way to know the demand. Make your best guess for the materials needed and the initial amount of product to make based on similar products, interested wholesale accounts, and customer requests for the new product. After sales begin, move to a pull system to replenish the initial product you made for the launch.

Holiday or Seasonal Product and Raw Materials: Push
No one is ordering your Valentine's Day line in January, but you're working on production then to get ready. Make your best guess based on last year's sales, planned marketing efforts, growth of other seasonal products since last year or the overall growth of your business. For quick-to-make products, start with a small amount and go to a pull system after the seasonal product has launched, just like any other new product launch. If it takes longer to make the product than the season lasts (slow-brewing beers

Bins for products

or handmade soaps that cure for more than six weeks, for example), make your best guess for the product demand for the season.

Checklist: Pull Systems

☐ Consider your daily activities and how you replenish stock of your materials and finished products. Where in your studio do you use a push approach? Where do you use a pull approach? Can you use a pull system more often?

☐ Follow this order of tasks for a few days in your studio. Does it help you view your activities as a pull system instead of a push system?
  - First, fill customer orders (see Chapter 10).
  - Next, refill any empty finished product and empty WIP bins (see Chapter 11).
  - Last, reorder any raw materials below materials reserve (see Chapters 12 and 13).

Next Up: Filling Orders
Sales orders are the source of all the activities in your studio. Filling orders is the first item that's part of your pull system.

CHAPTER 10 – FILLING ORDERS

All your other studio activities are support for filling orders. Get your product out the door and into the hands of a customer.

You'll need:
   -Customer orders to fill.

Orders Come First in a Pull System

Filling customer orders is the most important activity in your studio. Filling orders comes first in a pull system because every other activity at the studio is done to support filling orders. Production activities, storage and ordering of raw materials is all done to respond to customer orders.

IN-PERSON SALES AND FULFILLMENT

Selling Products in Person

The simplest way to fill an order is directly between you and your customer. You set up a table or display, and a customer pays via cash, check, or credit card. Temporary selling events include farmer's markets, craft shows, art fairs, and festivals. You also may operate your own semi-permanent or permanent retail location at your studio, a storefront, popup shop, or mall kiosk. Filling the order happens as the sale is made.

For orders not made in person, you'll have to track the open orders, pick and pack them, and ship/deliver them to the customer.

TRACKING OPEN ORDERS

Track All Your Sales Channels

Each different way customers can order your products is a sales channel. Your own ecommerce site is one sales channel. Third-party listing sites— such as Etsy, Ebay, Facebook, and Amazon—are sales channels. Direct emails or phone calls from wholesale customers to place orders are sales channels. Make a list of the ways you allow people to place orders. Do you have a central place to keep all your open orders so you can track and fulfill them in a reasonable time?

Keep a Single List of Open Orders

Compile all open orders into a trackable list to ensure everything has been accounted for. Some online fulfillment software systems, such as Shippo or ShipStation, automatically compile different orders into a single list you also can add to manually, as needed. A whiteboard also can be used to track orders, or orders can be printed and the stack of paper used as a working list of open orders.

Set Aside Time for Fulfillment

Fill orders at the same time each day or week, which helps you track how much time you're spending on order fulfillment. Because specialized knowledge of making your products isn't needed to fill orders, it's often one of the first tasks product makers hire someone to complete. By knowing the time spent on fulfillment, you can more easily estimate how much help you need, or whether you need an external fulfillment service. If you are following a daily production schedule, start with the "pull" of customer orders in the morning, which allows the rest of production tasks to follow the rest of the day.

Set Aside Space for Fulfillment

Use a dedicated space for filling orders. This can be a 100% dedicated table or one that is cleared off when it's time to fill orders. For a multiuse location, use the activity kit system described in Chapter 5 to keep your filling and packing materials ready to go. Anything you need to pack orders should be added to this kit/station. To start, here are some things to have ready when filling orders:

- Computer and printer for printing packing slips, invoices, and shipping labels
- Trays for collecting and separating ordered items
- Packing filler material, such as paper or peanuts
- Tape, Scissors, Pens, Markers
- Boxes for shipping
- Thank-you notes, samples, or other extras, such as stickers telling customers you reuse packing materials

PICK AND PACK

What Is Picking and Packing?

Picking and packing is the process of gathering finished products into one place to fill a customer order. The completed order will be shipped to or picked up by the customer. This consists of two separate activities: picking/gathering the items needed, and packing them for shipping or pickup.

Packing Slips

Packing slips are printed copies of customer orders that are packed with the items. A packing slip tells you what to pick and allows you to double check the order while packing. The packing slip also tells the customer what is inside the package. Creating a packing slip can be done manually or using a template from your fulfillment software. You also can use a printed copy of a customer order as a packing slip. If you print a packing slip for each order placed, use the pile of packing slips as your to-do list while filling orders. This helps ensure every order gets filled.

Typically, the following information is included on the packing slip:

- Customer identification (name, address).
- Order identification (order number, date, purchase order number).
- Products ordered.
- Quantity ordered.
- Store contact information (name, phone number, email, address).
- Shipping information (service).
- Information needed for customer service issues, such as a return policy

Packing Slip

Order #123
Order Date: 1/1/2010

Recipient:	Shipper:
Erika Williams	Amazing Almonds
45 Walnut Drive	97 Industrial Drive
Springfield, Alaska 10012	Nicetown, California 18793

Item Details

QTY	SKU	Description
1	RA-012	Raw Almonds, 12 oz
2	RS-012	Roasted and Salted Almonds, 12 oz
1	FS-012	Five-Spice Roasted Almonds, 12 oz

Shipping Method: USPS Priority

Order Picked By: _____
Order Packed By:_____

Thank you for your business!

Return Policy: All sales are final. Please contact customer service at 555-1234
if you have any issues with your order.

Figure 10-1. Packing Slip

Pick First

Separating the two steps of picking and packing helps verify the order is correct. Using the packing slip as a checklist, the order is collected from storage/warehousing. The person who picks the order should initial the "picked by" line on the packing slip.

Packing Slip
Order #123
Order Date: 1/1/2010

Recipient:	Shipper:
Erika Williams	Amazing Almonds
45 Walnut Drive	97 Industrial Drive
Springfield, Alaska 10012	Nicetown, California 18793

Item Details

QTY	SKU	Description
1	RA-012	Raw Almonds, 12 oz
2	RS-012	Roasted and Salted Almonds, 12 oz
1	FS-012	Five-Spice Roasted Almonds, 12 oz

Shipping Method: USPS Priority

Order Picked By: ___RS___

Order Packed By: _____

Thank you for your business!

Return Policy: All sales are final. Please contact customer service at 555-1234 if you have any issues with your order.

Figure 10-2. Packing Slip is Signed after Picking

Separate Orders Visually

The picked order is laid out on a table, in a box, on a tray or other contained area along with the packing slip. Using a physical space like a piece of paper or the sides of a tray helps visually separate orders from one another.

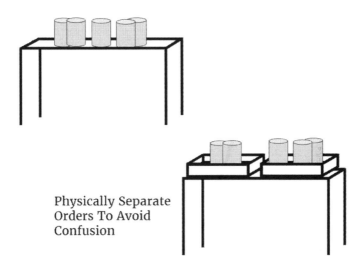

Physically Separate
Orders To Avoid
Confusion

Figure 10-3. Visually Separated Orders

Flag Orders That Are Not Ready to Ship
Use a visual flag/alert system to identify any orders that are not ready to ship. The orders might have special requirements, such as samples to be added, a personal note to write, or product that needs to be made before the order ships. The needs–attention flag should be something simple yet visually out of place, such as a brightly colored gift-wrapping bow, a mini traffic cone, or a yellow rubber duck. By easily identifying any order that needs special attention, you can focus on moving out all the other orders without worrying that you will accidentally pack an order before it is complete.

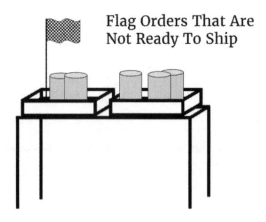

Figure 10–4. Flagged Order

Pack the Order

To pack, take a completed picked order and check it against the packing slip. Ideally, one person picks the order and a second person checks it while packing. You also can pick orders in the morning and pack in the afternoon, checking them yourself. Seeing each order twice gives you a chance to catch any mistakes in product quantity or type. When checking and packing, place your initials on the "packed by" location on the packing slip.

Packing Slip
Order #123
Order Date: 1/1/2010

Recipient:	Shipper:
Erika Williams	Amazing Almonds
45 Walnut Drive	97 Industrial Drive
Springfield, Alaska 10012	Nicetown, California 18793

Item Details

QTY	SKU	Description
1	RA-012	Raw Almonds, 12 oz
2	RS-012	Roasted and Salted Almonds, 12 oz
1	FS-012	Five-Spice Roasted Almonds, 12 oz

Shipping Method: USPS Priority

Order Picked By: ___RS___
Order Packed By: ___JB___

Thank you for your business!

Return Policy: All sales are final. Please contact customer service at 555-1234 if you have any issues with your order.

Figure 10-5. Packing Slip is Signed during Packing

Ship the Order

The outside of the package should contain enough information to get the order to the right place and avoid confusion with other orders. For shipping using a common carrier such as UPS, USPS, FedEx, or DHL, the shipping label will contain this information. If using a trucking company, delivering yourself, or having customers pick up, include—at a minimum—the customer name and order number.

```
Amazing Almonds
97 Industrial Drive
Nicetown, California 18793    Order #843


Customer:                    Shipping Method:
                             Direct Delivery to Store
Nicetown Health Shoppe       Receiving Hours:
423 Retail Store Lane        6a–1p M–Sat
Nicetown, CA 18793


Customer PO Number: 2062345
Order Date: 1/1/2020
```

Figure 10-6. Example Label To Identify Order For Delivery

Alert the Customer

Send tracking information to your customer so they know to expect the package. Many shipping services will allow you to send automated emails with this information when the shipping labels are created.

USING OUTSIDE FULFILLMENT SERVICES

Third Party Fulfillment Companies

There are many services available that store your products and fill customer orders on your behalf. Rather than hiring someone to come to your studio and fill orders, you hire the fulfillment service to accept large shipments of your product and pick, pack, ship, and send notifications to your customers from a separate warehouse location. There are a growing number of ecommerce fulfillment companies offering such services. Because fulfillment companies hire dedicated workers to pick and pack orders, and receive volume discounts on shipping costs, they can potentially fulfill orders more efficiently than each individual business. However, after considering the markup of these costs, the final cost to you often is the same or more than fulfilling directly. Some popular fulfillment services in the United States are FedEx Fulfillment, Amazon, and WhiteBox.

Fulfillment Service Costs

The direct monetary cost of using a fulfillment service includes setup fees, storage fees, per-order costs, inventory receiving fees, and more. There also is the cost of losing an opportunity for you to interact with your customers through the "unboxing" experience. Because of the time needed to send product to the fulfillment service, you would need to keep more inventory on hand at the fulfillment center than you would if filling orders directly from your studio.

Fulfillment Service Benefits

Benefits to using a fulfillment service include eliminating a large space-consuming and time-consuming activity from your operations so you can focus on other things. If your studio is low on space, send product to the fulfillment center as it's produced and use all the available space for production activities. If you don't yet have a production facility, rent temporary space (at a shared commercial kitchen perhaps) and produce enough inventory to send to the fulfillment center, then manage your business from home. This allows you to scale up without any dedicated studio space.

DISTRIBUTORS

Distributors Are Logistics Partners

Distributors warehouse products and ship them to stores. When you sell product to a retail store that in turn sells to customers, you can either manage each store's inventory and fill orders yourself or use a distributor. Essentially, a distributor is an outside fulfillment company that specializes in sending products to businesses for resale. If you aren't sure what distributors potentially carry your products, ask the buyer at a retail store where your products are sold or where you want your products to be sold. The buyer will know the commonly used distributors in your industry.

Cost of Using Distributors

Distributors require an existing customer demand for your product. The distributor will charge various fees—both directly and a percentage of sales cost—for the services it provides, such as warehousing and shipping. Sales support typically is not included in the percentage fees taken by distributors, so a brand must provide its own sales staff or pay the distributor for this additional service. Distributors in different industries work differently and have different requirements and costs, so the best way to learn more is to contact the distributors used in your industry.

Benefits of Distributors

Distributors provide services such as warehousing and shipping product to stores. They are convenient for stores because the buyer can purchase stock from a single catalog rather than individual manufacturers. Many stores prefer this convenience, so using a distributor increases the number of stores willing to carry your product. They also provide support, such as product information, sales promotion support, and demo/sampling services. Using these services can be a simple way to expand the capabilities of the sales function at your company without adding more people to your staff.

Checklist: Fulfillment

☐ Compile your sales channels.
   - o Make a list of all the ways you allow customers to order from you.
   - o Make sure each order gets tracked and fulfilled using your process.

☐ Set up picking, packing, and shipping for your products.
   - o Create your packing list template for filling orders.
   - o Set up space in your studio to fill orders.
   - o Fill orders at the same time each day or week and track how much time you spend on order fulfillment.
   - o Consider an outside fulfillment company or a distributor to grow your order fulfillment capability.

Up Next: Production Scheduling

After filling orders, work to refill your product inventory by making more finished products.

CHAPTER 11 – PRODUCTION SCHEDULING

Make product to match customer orders. Adopt a kanban, or bin, system to make production automatic and take away decision-making for what to make each day.

You'll need:
-Trays, bins, or boxes of a consistent size.
-Labels, markers, and colored tape to label bins.
-Notes on the current batch size for each of your products.
-Notes on approximate sales rates of each of your products.

WHAT IS KANBAN?

Definition of Kanban

Like many manufacturing terms, the word "kanban" comes from Japanese production systems. The word translates roughly to "visible sign", meaning a card or billboard. Using kanban means you will use some type of physical sign to tell the production team what to make. This can be done with a written card, writing on a whiteboard, or physically moving an empty cart or bin in the studio.

Kanban Card, Bin, Tray, Hopper?

When using this system, you can call your kanban any term that makes sense to you. Any container, such as a bin, box or tray can be labeled on the outside with information. Cards can be attached to large items. Since the word "bin" is familiar and can refer to many different sizes, we'll use this term to refer to the containers used in the kanban system.

A Two-Bin System: A Backup Battery for Production

When you are worried about the battery running out on your phone, a cordless drill, or your digital camera, you keep a backup battery handy. When the first battery runs out of power, you grab the backup battery and recharge the spent battery. This way, your project keeps moving while the extra battery recharges.

You can apply the same technique to materials in your studio. You work to fill orders by pulling items from one bin. When you get to the end of the bin, it's time to restock. But you don't want to wait to continue filling orders, so you have a second bin that is used while the first bin is refilled. Having multiple bins means you never run out of product at the wrong time. When you reach the bottom of a bin, you start working on the next one while the empty bin is refilled.

In a bustling car factory, one person may be using a bin of parts to assemble items while another person fills empty bins from a central storage area. In a smaller studio, this bin system allows you to continue without interruption.

This way, you can complete any task, such as pulling a customer order, without being stopped by an inventory issue. You then refill the bins from inventory later.

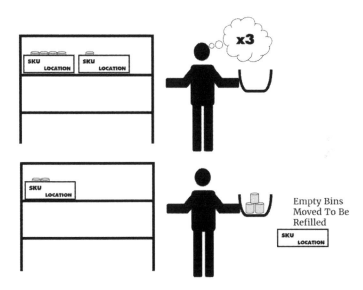

Figure 11-1. Pulling Multiple Items. Continue Pulling Product Once the First Bin is Empty.

RULES FOR BIN SYSTEMS

Toyota's Six Rules for Effective Kanban Systems
The kanban name and basics of using the system were developed for Toyota Motor Corporation, a large company with many employees and different departments. This same function also can be done very simply in the studio with one person and a set of bins and labels.

Bins for 12 products?

Kanban Rule One. Downstream/Customer stations withdraw items in the exact amounts specified by the kanban.

In your studio: When you move a full bin of product to a different part of the studio to be stored or used, you always know exactly how much you have because the bins are always filled to the size and quantity indicated. If the bin is full, there is no need to count or measure the items.

Kanban Rule Two. Upstream/Supplier stations produce items in the precise amounts and sequences specified by the kanban.

In your studio: Product gets made to fill the empty bins. Make product in the same size and quantity each time you have an empty bin. When filling a bin, fill it - don't under or overfill it. The number of items per bin and the number of bins is how the total amount of product is controlled.

Kanban Rule Three. No items are made or moved without a kanban.

In your studio: Don't make product unless your system needs it, as indicated by an empty bin. If a bin is half-filled, leave it half-filled. Only refill it once it's completely empty.

Kanban Rule Four. A kanban should accompany every item.

In your studio: Product should never be unlabeled or sitting outside a bin. Product should not be made without a bin, which contains important information about the product and quantity needed.

Kanban Rule Five. Defects are never sent to the next process.

In your studio: Never place a product with a problem in a bin. If defective products stay in the bin, your next process won't have the right number of correct items. Defective products should be flagged immediately, removed from the production floor, and dealt with separate from regular production.

Kanban Rule Six. The number of kanbans is reduced carefully to lower inventories.

In your studio: When sales levels are consistent, reducing the number of bins is a good way to reduce inventory levels. This improves cash flow and increases production speed. In a studio where sales levels are growing (and often growing quickly), however, it's more common to add bins than to take them away. Reducing bins is recommended when sales level off or if you're working to reduce the total inventory you have on hand (see Chapter 12). A good time to reduce bins is when seasonal products are getting to the end of their sales cycle. Reduce the end-of-season items as you add bins to the next season's inventory to properly allocate space – and cash – where it should go.

WHY USE BINS TO MAKE AND MOVE PRODUCTS?

Bins Make Your Pull System Happen
In a pull system, everything starts with a customer order. Using bins helps control the flow of production so product can quickly be moved to fill orders, then the WIP and inventory can be restocked to the appropriate levels.

Bins Control Production Speed and Inventory Levels
A working bin system makes sure you have just enough inventory on hand to keep your pull system moving. As soon as a customer places an order, they receive an item from inventory. Then the factory builds more of that item, builds WIP needed for the item, and reorders any raw materials needed, working backwards through the system to ensure the entire system is ready to go for the next order.

The exact amount of product moved depends on the batch sizes and customer demand. This system can change over time as the studio adjusts batch sizes and has changes in sales volume.

Only the Amount Needed
Bins deliver items only when they are ready to be sold or used by the next customer, eliminating excessive pileup of inventory or finished products on

the floor or in the warehouse. Using bins is a way to regulate product flow through the factory. Think of it as a system of pipes that you control so you can increase or reduce how much material heads to a certain place.

What Should You Make Today?

How do you decide what product to make on any given day in the studio? With limited time, making the wrong thing hurts twice: You don't want to make product that isn't selling, and you don't have time to waste when you have orders to get out the door. By using this system, your to-do list is entirely out of your hands and controlled by your customer. There's no need to calculate what needs to be made—you simply visit the area where empty bins are kept and see what needs replenishment.

All the time previously spent on production scheduling can now be used for other things. Creating a to-do list is not necessary, and you and any employees in the studio can tell what needs to be done by looking at the empty bins.

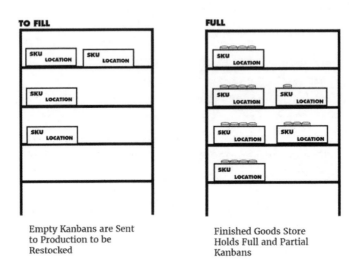

Empty Kanbans are Sent
to Production to be
Restocked

Finished Goods Store
Holds Full and Partial
Kanbans

Figure 11-2. The storage rack on the left, empty bins, is your visual to-make list.

The End of Your To-Make List

In your studio, you are used to having an endless list of things that need doing. The very best thing about using bins as your production scheduling system is your production to-make list no longer is infinite. After your bins are refilled, you're done with production. Then you wait for orders to come in and when they pull enough product out to create empty bins, you start again.

SETTING UP AND USING BINS

Information to Include on Your Bin

Because your bin is the signal that you need to make more product, include enough information on it to tell you exactly what needs to be made. Information to include on your bins includes:

- Product name
- Quantity per bin
- Storage location for the full bin
- Return location for the empty bin

Figure 11-3. Labeled Bin

Increasing Speed to Refill Bins
Using this bin system works whether you have one production day a month or week, or whether you're making product every day. You may go from refilling a bin once a month to once a week to once a day. If you increase how often you make product, you can keep the same number of bins as you move from hobby, to side business, to full time.

When Your Product 'Doesn't Work' With Bins
Using bin to control production scheduling works best with steady demand for product and a pull system. For situations where a pull system doesn't work well (seasonal product, special orders, new product launches), use temporary bins for orders as needed. The easiest method for managing this is a printed or handwritten order attached to a bin. This maintains the system of picking up a bin to get a job.

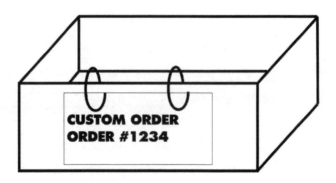

Figure 11-4. Using Bins for Custom Orders

Order of Refilling Bins
Because everything starts with a customer order, prioritize customer orders first. After all orders are filled, refilling bins is the next activity, and so on back up the line of your product line using the pull system.

How Big Should Your Bins Be and How Many Should You Have?

Because your bins act as backup batteries to run your production, you can control how long your production runs are by changing how big the bins are and how many you have.

The number and size of bins is not meant to be permanent—it should shift over time, just as your order size and frequency does.

Basic Two-Bin System

The simplest approach is to have two bins of each item. The bin contains a single batch of your product. No adjustments or calculations are needed to use this two-bin system. You'll fill orders from the first bin, and when you run out you keep working using the second bin.

The empty bin tells you it's time to make a new batch—move it to a separate area you have set aside for empty bins. The new batch fills the bin, and the full bin is ready to take over when the current bin is emptied.

Calculating the Number of Bins

If you're growing quickly, or want to be a little more accurate, you can calculate the precise number of bins you need for an item. To calculate the right number of bins for your studio, consider several additional factors:

$$B = \frac{S \times T}{Q} + 1$$

B: Number of bins needed for this product.

S: Sales per week of the product.

T: Time—in weeks—needed to restock an empty bin. Include any required safety time.

Q: Quantity or amount of product in each bin. For simplicity, start with a single batch size.

Example 1: Lip Balm

Lip balm is made in batches of 24 balms. There are 20 sales per week. You produce this item once a week. So, Q = 24, S = 20, and T = 1

B = ((20×1)/24) +1 = (20/24) +1 = 1.83

Rounding up to the nearest whole number, you need two bins for lip balm.

Example 2: Headbands

You make 25 headbands at a time. You have 100 sales per week. You make headbands every few days, so you need about half a week to restock. So, Q = 25, S = 100, and T = 0.5

B = (100×0.5)/25 + 1 = (50/25) + 1 = 3.

You need three bins for headbands.

Checklist: Production Scheduling

☐ Identify which products should be auto-replenished when sold. These products will be set up with bins.

☐ Calculate your starting bin size and number of bins.

☐ Label bins with item information.

☐ Establish an area to put empty bins to be filled, creating a visual to-make list.

Up Next: Inventory Management

Keeping the right amount of product on hand.

CHAPTER 12 – INVENTORY

How much product do you, and should you, keep on hand?

You'll need:
-Inventory counts and values from your accounting system or physical inventory.
-Cost of goods sold value from your accounting system.
-List of important raw materials you order.
-Information on past orders of raw materials: date ordered, amount, and supplier.
-Notes on your sales volume for various products.

WHY MANAGE INVENTORY?

Inventory: Can't Live With It, Can't Live Without It
You need inventory, but not too much! It is listed as an asset on balance sheets, and it's necessary to make and sell your products. But inventory also ties up valuable cash and floor space, limiting their use.

Think of inventory as a set of gift cards—money that's yours, but of limited usefulness. When the gift card is purchased, it immediately changes from cash in your pocket to credit that's only useful in some ways. You can't use a Starbucks gift card, for example, to pay your electric bill, and you can't use materials inventory to pay rent or invest in equipment. Therefore, the decision to spend resources on inventory should be made carefully, avoiding excess whenever possible.

MEASURING INVENTORY

When counting and managing inventory, use a physical count of all items— the actual amount you have on hand. You also can use a calculation of your virtual inventory, or the inventory you have on paper, which is calculated based on what you've purchased and what you've sold. You'll likely use virtual and physical inventory systems in different ways at your studio.

Using Virtual Inventory
In an inventory management system, purchases of raw materials are added as inputs and materials are calculated as outputs as they are made into products and sold. The remaining inventory is calculated, and the amount of raw materials can be checked at any time without physically measuring the remaining stock. A virtual inventory can be as simple as a handwritten ledger, an electronic spreadsheet, or a materials use sheet stored with your materials.

Software solutions for managing virtual inventory are available but may not be useful or worth the expense, especially for smaller businesses. QuickBooks or Xero for accounting, along with related plugins like Unleashed are designed to help manage your inventory. There also are industry-specific software options like Craftybase or SoapMaker3.

Even if you use software, you'll need to choose a point for reordering and can use the calculations below to pick your restock points. You may find it helpful to use physical signs and reorder flags on the floor so you aren't running from the factory floor to your computer to check what's going on.

The Upside of Using Software to Manage Inventory
With a software program, you can see everything in one place from your desk. It's easy to summarize your financials at tax time.

The Downside of Using Software to Manage Inventory
Software programs have a one-time or ongoing expense. The virtual inventory is not always accurate. If you haven't included all potential uses of inventory product in the system, your inventory system will not account for all the product you use, and you could run out in the studio despite seeing plenty of stock available on your computer.

Using Physical Inventory
A physical count of all inventory items in your studio should be taken at regular intervals. If you use virtual inventory for managing your day-to-day decisions and financial reports, a physical count typically is done at least once per year. Adjustments to the virtual inventory are made after the physical inventory count so the virtual inventory system reflects the actual amount of product on hand.

It's best to do a physical inventory during the slowest part of the year. Close the studio and pause most other production and selling activities for the day to get through it at quickly as possible and avoid double-counting or missing items that are sold or made that day. A scale—especially with a count function—helps with small items that are difficult to count individually. A handheld tally counter also can help make the inventory count go faster.

Calculating Inventory Turns

Inventory amount is measured in turns. Select a time frame—typically one year—and use the following formula for calculating turns:

$$Inventory\ turns = \frac{Cost\ of\ goods\ sold}{Average\ inventory}$$

Cost of Goods Sold (COGS)

COGS is the actual money spent on materials that have been sold as product. Do not include labor costs. How much of your inventory has departed as sellable product in this time?

Average Inventory

To get the average on-hand inventory, add the value of your inventory at the start of the time period (January 1) to the value at the end (December 31) and divide by 2.

Example Inventory Calculation

A dog treat baking company had $10,000 in ingredients on January 1 and $15,000 on December 31. Over the course of the year, the dog treats sold included $125,000 in materials.

> Starting Inventory = $10,000
> Ending Inventory = $15,000
> Average Inventory = ($10,000 + $15,000)/2 = $25,000/2 = $12,500
> Cost of Goods Sold (COGS) = $125,000

Inventory Turns = $125,000/$12,500 = 10

In a single year, this company turned over inventory 10 times.

WHAT IS THE RIGHT NUMBER OF INVENTORY TURNS?

Industries Vary

A juice company, with lots of fresh ingredients, should have higher turnover than a jewelry maker, which can hold raw materials for years. For comparing your own inventory turns, it's best to find other companies with a similar product.

A higher number of inventory turns represents a company that's more efficient at buying materials and turning them into sellable product. In general, increasing your inventory turns is a good thing.

Changing Your Inventory Turns

If you want to increase or decrease your inventory turns, change the amount and frequency of materials purchases. Your number of inventory turns is related to your purchasing strategy. A three-month purchase aim correlates to four inventory turns a year. If you aim for six months, that's two turns per year. The more of your items you purchase in the target time frame, the closer you'll be to your target inventory turnover.

If you are aiming for 12 turns per year, that represents all new inventory every month. Some items may be very difficult to purchase at that cadence and some may be easy. If there are products with a short and reliable delivery time, purchase these more often and in smaller amounts to decrease your inventory.

Responsible Inventory Management: Aim for Your Own Target

The amount of inventory you keep on hand is a strategic choice based on your industry, space, cash considerations, and customer needs. Lean manufacturing consultants often say you should strive for zero inventory. This is called "just in time" inventory management. This kind of system has you constantly hitting your materials reserve and ordering a small amount very frequently. For a small manufacturing company without a dedicated purchasing team, constantly ordering and managing product inventory is unrealistic. Instead, decide on an inventory level that's appropriate for your business and look for ways to reduce it over time.

DON'T RUN OUT: HOLDING A MATERIALS RESERVE

Reorder Materials Before You Run Out

When you place an order to restock materials, you need enough on hand to last you until your order arrives. The amount you need to keep on hand depends on how quickly you use materials and how long it takes for new orders to arrive.

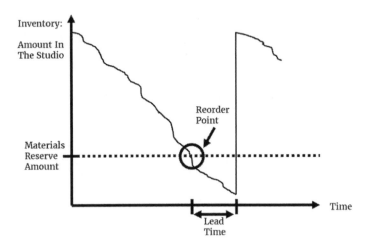

Figure 12-1. Inventory Management Curve

Materials Reserve: Your Low-Fuel Light

Your materials reserve is a cushion to let you know you are running low on an item and it's time to reorder. Think of this reserve amount like the low-fuel light on a car. If you hit the reserve, you know it's time to plan for restocking. You don't want to find out you're out of fuel in the middle of a commute, and you don't want to discover you're out of a key ingredient in the middle of filling a customer order.

Holding a Virtual Reserve

Set the reserve point in your software system. For spreadsheets, color-code cells to change color below your reserve line. With an inventory software system, set an alert for products that fall below the reserve or have new purchase orders automated and sent to suppliers.

Physically Separate Your Reserve

Make it very clear when you begin using your reserve materials. You can create a flag or sign on the last bundle of cardboard boxes. Better, move the last bundle of boxes to a totally separate storage area. Use a sign like the one in Figure 12-2 to make it easy to separate your reserve amount from the rest of your inventory. When you remove the sign, you will know you've started using your reserve and it's time to reorder.

Do Not Open Without Reordering

Item Details	Ordering Details
Part:	Supplier:
Description:	Lead Time:
	Qty in Reserve:

Figure 12-2. Hold Sign Placed on Product Reserve

Calcuating Your Materials Reserve Size

Your Materials Reserve size depending on how long it takes to restock the material and how much material you use. As you await the arrival of your new materials, production continues. Your reserve must have enough product to supply your production needs during this time.

Materials Reserve = Materials Use Per Week x Lead Time in Weeks

What's the Lead Time?

Lead time for restocking materials is the total time that passes from when you know you need to reorder a material until it's in your studio ready to use. Suppliers may tell you they have a certain lead time, which may or may not include shipping or order processing time. Add up the total time needed for all the following items:

$$Total\ Lead\ Time = L1 + L2 + L3 + L4$$

L1: Time it takes to place an order after you know you need to restock.
You might place orders once per day or once per week. Include the time it takes to gather information about what supplier to buy from, how many to buy, and any time needed to prepare a Purchase Order or place an order using your supplier's system.

L2: Time from order placement until your supplier has the product ready.
Typically, this is the lead time your supplier will quote when asked.

L3: Transit Time
How long does the product take to get from the supplier to you? The location of the supplier and shipping service used are the main contributors to this time. For local pickup, this is the time it takes to go and get the item.

L4: Receiving Time
How long it takes to receive the material into your system. This includes getting the product to the right place and ready to use and any necessary cleaning or conditioning, such as allowing the material to come to ambient temperature from storage.

Total Lead Time
Total lead times vary from a few minutes (for picking something up off the shelf at a nearby grocery store) to a few weeks or even months (for custom-made product requiring overseas shipping).

Re-calculate Materials Reserve Amounts As Needed
Revisit these calculations regularly. As your production volume grows, your reserve size will grow as well. Hitting your materials reserve more often and reordering more frequently is an indication your reserve should go up and/or your ordering size should increase.

Checklist: Inventory Management

☐ Take a physical inventory and update your virtual inventory system, if used.

☐ Calculate your inventory turns and compare to similar businesses.

☐ Make a list of your critical materials in inventory.

☐ Calculate reserve amounts for these critical materials.

☐ Create signs for the critical items and place them on your physical reserve in your studio. Add reordering points into your electronic or virtual inventory system.

Up Next: Purchasing and Supply Chain
When you're ready to restock your inventory, you need the right materials, at the right time, in the right amount for the right price.

CHAPTER 13 – PURCHASING AND SUPPLIERS

A reliable supply chain helps ensure you have the materials you need, when you need them, in the right amounts for the right price.

You'll need:
−A list of your current suppliers.
−A list of your important purchased items.

WHY FOCUS ON PURCHASING?

Costs Are Half of Your Profit Equation
You've likely heard the phrase, "A dollar saved is a dollar earned." Large organizations have teams dedicated entirely to purchasing and supply chain. It's common for these professionals to save the company multiples of their salary each year, showing there is a great return on investment for paying close and constant attention to this part of your business. Even a once-per-year evaluation of current suppliers, ordering quantities, and possible alternatives helps reduce costs.

THE RIGHT MATERIALS

Purchasing and Technical Specifications
Do you know the technical details on the materials you buy? Is your baking soda USP Grade #1 or USP Grade #2? What particle size is the sugar used in your bakery? What type of lamination is used on your product labels? What diameter is the wire used in your jewelry? Using specifications helps to ensure your ingredients and components—and therefore your finished products—stay consistent over time as you make multiple purchases or change suppliers.

Documenting Your Specifications
When buying a new item, look or ask for a technical data sheet or specification sheet, and keep this information on file. If your supplier provides testing information such as a certificate of analysis, file that as well. If you need to find a different source for your purchases in the future, use these filed reports to compare the materials and determine whether you will purchase the same item from the new supplier.

TCC The Coconut Co
35 Coconut Drive
Supplierville, NJ 97415

Technical Data Sheet

Product: Organic Coconut Oil RBD
Product Codes: 12345, 23456, 34567
Sources: Sri Lanka, Phillipines

Ingredients: **Certifications:**
Organic Coconut   Organic, Kosher, Fair Trade

Packaging/Size Options: **Storage Requirements:**
30 lb pail   <70% relative humidity
400 lb drum (steel)   <70 degrees Fahrenheit
2000 lb totle

Analytical Properties

Attribute	Method	Range
Aroma	Organoleptic	None
Flavor	Organoleptic	Bland
Free Fatty Acids %	AOCS Ca	<0.10
Saponification Value	AOCS Cd	250–264
Iodine Value	AOCS Cd	6.0–11.0

last update: January 1, 2020

Figure 13-1. Technical Data Sheet

TCC

The Coconut Co
35 Coconut Drive
Supplierville, NJ 97415

Certificate of Analysis

Product: Organic Coconut Oil RBD
Product Number: 12345
Production Date: January 1, 2020
Shelf Life: 18 months from production
Lot Number: 988766
Manufactured In: Sri Lanka

Attribute	Method	Range	Results	Pass/Fail
Aroma	Organoleptic	None	None	PASS
Flavor	Organoleptic	Bland	Bland	PASS
Free Fatty Acids %	AOCS Ca	<0.10	0.02	PASS
Saponification Value	AOCS Cd	250–264	258	PASS
Iodine Value	AOCS Cd	6.0–11.0	8.2	PASS

Feb 12, 2020

Technician: Marie Curie
QA Department, TCC

Date

Figure 13-2. Certificate of Analysis

Internal Product Requirements

Using the information from items you bought previously is a good start when looking for suppliers. You also may come up with your own requirements for your purchases. Keep this information on file and handy when looking for new suppliers.

Consider both quality and cost when documenting your product requirements. If you are making food products, you don't want to purchase industrial-grade baking soda. If you are making cosmetics, you don't want to purchase pharmaceutical-grade citric acid.

Product Requirements

Product: Coconut Oil
Company Part Number: P0012

REQUIREMENTS

Certifications: Organic, Kosher, Fair Trade
COAs provided for each lot; Nutrition Information reported

PREFERENCES

Processing: Refined, Bleached, Deodorized (RBD)
Environmentally Preferable Supplier
Supplied in 400-lb Steel Drum Sizes

SUPPLIERS

Preferred: The Coconut Company
Secondary: Tropical Oils Galore, SuperOilSupply

last update: January 1, 2020 by Brenda Buyer

Figure 13-3. Product Requirements

Incoming Inspection of Purchases

When purchases arrive, always inspect the incoming product right away. If there is a problem, it's easier to fix it early instead of waiting until you're about to use it in production. Use a check sheet like the one below when receiving and inspecting items.

For a complicated or custom item, you may have multiple items to check, such as color match, size, and weight. For other items you may simply check that the item appears to be the right one and hasn't been mixed up with a different order. The information from your incoming inspection sheet can be transferred into your software or accounting program, or simply stored as reference.

Incoming Inspection Sheet

Product: Glass Bottle, 16oz
Company Part Number: P0056

Requirement	Method	Pass/Fail
Brown Glass	Visual	
Weight <9oz	Lab Scale	
Correct # Delivered	Check against PO	

Inspected By: _____ **Date:** _____

Figure 13-4. Incoming Inspection Sheet

THE RIGHT AMOUNT

It's Time to Reorder—Now What?

In Chapter 12, all stock levels, reserves, and reordering points are based on the amount you actually use in your studio. The minimum amount on hand is based on how much gets used. But what about the maximum amount, or the quantity to buy when you're restocking? When you purchase items, how to do you know how much to buy?

Should You Buy in Bulk?

The best working definition of bulk is: "More than you buy now." If you are starting out, five pounds of an ingredient may be a bulk purchase to you. A larger company would consider a full pallet of 2,000 pounds to be a bulk purchase. Cost per unit decreases when the total amount purchased goes up—this is the main idea behind buying more to save money. However, larger purchases take up more space, tie up cash that could be used for other things, and drop the number of inventory turns. Instead of thinking of buying more, find the right amount of products to buy.

Minimum Order Quantity (MOQ)

MOQ is the term for the minimum allowable order size from your supplier. This can vary—some suppliers let you buy a single item while others require full cases, pallets, or truckloads to be purchased at a time. Finding a supplier with an MOQ that matches your needs helps avoid overspending on inventory and buying too much.

Actual Order Quantity

You will include cost savings from bulk discounts, shipping, and other considerations to determine the order size for your company for a single product from a supplier. To strike a balance between discounts for larger purchases and keeping your inventory low to keep more cash on hand, base your purchase size on your desired amount of inventory. If your target number of inventory turns is four times per year, you want to buy three months of materials each time. Your supplier may ship for a flat fee, which reduces your per-piece cost on larger orders, or there may be a discount applied to larger orders. If your target is enough material for three months of use, also consider a range of between two and four months. Select your order size based on the lowest total pricing for order quantities in this range.

Example: Buying Scoops
You use 10,000 Scoops in three months and the MOQ is 5,000. There are no price breaks until you purchase 50,000 – over a year's worth. Purchase 10,000 scoops.

Example: Buying Boxes
You use one pallet of boxes per month. There is a 20% price break at four pallets, so you buy four months' worth to receive the discount.

THE RIGHT TIME

Supplier Lead Time
Arrival time for your purchases can have a big effect on how much you buy at once and how frequently you buy. It's one of the important parts of calculating the amount of reserve material you keep on hand (see Chapter 12). Finding suppliers that can deliver faster allows you to keep a smaller reserve on hand. If you know your items will arrive the next day, buy a smaller amount at a time and repurchase when you run out.

You probably do not keep a reserve of office supplies because you know you can purchase a pen or printer paper on a moment's notice. Your custom product packaging takes longer to obtain, though, so it requires more planning. If your sales are increasing, you may have trouble meeting unexpected orders unless you have suppliers that can get your purchases to you quickly.

THE RIGHT PRICE

Ask for Discounts

If you are buying the same materials repeatedly from the same supplier, that supplier wants to keep you around. It's worth it to ask for a price reevaluation every so often. Call or send a note similar to the one below to let the supplier know you are looking at pricing and give them an opportunity to offer you any adjustments or discounts.

Hello Packaging R Us Team,

I'm updating our cost files and want to check in with you about 10" Cube Boxes, item #1234. We bought 20,000 of these last year and are expecting to continue to use you as our primary supplier this year. We expect to buy 30,000 in the coming year. Can you check to make sure we're getting your best pricing for this item? We usually order 5,000 units per PO. Are there quantity discounts available near this purchase amount?

Best, Brenda the Buyer

Figure 13-5. Supplier Communication Example

Payment Terms

What terms are you paying with suppliers, and what do you get from customers? How much time elapses between when you spend $1 for raw material and when you receive $2 from the product you made with it? If your supplier requires cash on order and delivers in a week, it takes three weeks to make the product and your customer has net 30 terms—that's 60 days from the time you buy something to when you see the cash come back.

_ad, if you use a supplier that extends net 30 payment terms to you, *and* if they accept a credit card, that's nearly 60 days from when you receive materials to when you pay for them, which is the same time frame you're receiving payment from your customer.

SUPPLIER SELECTION

Finding and Evaluating Suppliers

The best supplier is one that meets your needs on all the above topics: the right amount of the right product to you at the right time for the right price. Typically, three areas are used to assess suppliers: quality, cost, and speed. Make a quick assessment of your current suppliers for a single item using these items, as shown in the Preferred Supplier Chart below.

Table 13–1. Preferred Supplier Chart

Supplier	Acme	Bates	Chip
Quality	+	+	−
Cost	−	+	+
Speed	+	−	+
Preferred?	YES	NO	NO

You also can make a more detailed assessment based on your own needs, with ratings such as yes/no or a numerical score from one to 10 in each category, to give an overall rating to the supplier. Here are some elements to include:

- Cost per item
- Payment terms
- Turnaround time
- Response time from supplier sales team
- Customer service issues addressed thoroughly
- Provides test data on each batch
- Environmentally friendly supplier

Table 13-2. Quantitative Supplier Assessment Chart

Supplier	Acme	Bates	Chip
Cost per item	8	8	4
Payment Terms	5	6	6
Turnaround Time	9	4	5
Response Time	5	5	5
Customer Service	8	7	6
Batch Test Data	8	8	8
Environmentally Friendly	7	5	7
Average Score	7.1	6.1	5.8
Preferred?	YES	NO	NO

What if You Only Have a Single Supplier?

What happens if your supplier is suddenly unresponsive or out of stock? For key ingredients, having a primary supplier and one or more secondary suppliers will keep your studio open if there is a problem.

Secondary suppliers might be more expensive or have poorer service, but an established short list of all qualified suppliers reduces the time it takes to establish a backup plan when an ingredient is not delivered as expected.

Update Your Supplier List Regularly

You may find that although you are getting acceptable service from your main supplier, a second supplier can provide better pricing or turnaround time. Pricing and service changes over time, so re-quoting your items and checking in with backup suppliers regularly (once per quarter or once per year) keeps your list up to date and may direct you to switch between suppliers when service or prices change significantly.

Checklist: Purchasing

☐ Establish your ideal number of inventory turns and select the target purchase size based on that. Three months' use is a common purchasing target.

☐ Make a list of your critical purchased items.

☐ For each critical item, establish the purchasing standards for that item and collect any technical data or specifications on that item.

☐ Determine the important supplier items you will use to rate your suppliers.

☐ Rate your current suppliers of critical items.

☐ Find additional suppliers for critical items and add them to your supplier list.

☐ Update your purchasing specifications and supplier list regularly.

THANK YOU

Test readers and content input: Ellowyn Isaacson of Foxen Canyon Soap Company, Angie Gallo of Elemental Blue. Janelle, Sara, Beth. Editing: Lindsay Dal Porto. Manufacturing-minded friends that were always up for a discussion or a plant tour: Amy, Nate, Kendall, Meena, Max, Kyle, Jaime, Rachel. Inspiration to share knowledge on continuous improvement: Bill. All of the above: Mike.

TERMS AND DEFINITIONS

5S: The five steps of Sort, Set in Order, Shine, Standardize, Sustain. These steps help to organize a space and keep things clean and orderly.

Bin: a container holding a pre-determined amount of materials.

COA: Certificate of Analysis. A report showing the results of one or more quality assessment tests performed on a material.

Commercial: A zoning term referring to an area that is used for business purposes. Usually commercial zoning is necessary for businesses that operate a retail storefront.

Distributor: a logistical partner that assists with warehousing and shipping products in exchange for fees and/or a percentage of sales.

Factory: common term for a manufacturing location. In this book, usually refers to a larger location with multiple employees.

Floor Plan: A paper, computer, or chalkboard/whiteboard drawing showing the current or potential location of various items in the studio.

Fulfillment: the act of completing a sales order by making the product sold and getting it to the customer.

Industrial: A zoning term relating to the manufacture of products. For warehousing, processing, and inventory operations, industrial zoning is often required. Usually industrial zones allow for more noise and traffic than other zoning areas. Usually industrial zoning is necessary for businesses that make and warehouse products.

Inventory: the amount of finished product, Work-In-Process, and raw materials on hand.

JIT: Just In Time. A lean manufacturing term referring to the goal and practice of keeping very little inventory on hand.

Kanban: A system of signaling production what needs to be made. Usually involves written cards, labeled bins, or other visual cues.

Layout: The location of various equipment, walkways, and work areas in the studio.

Lead Time: Amount of time it takes from an order is placed until it is fulfilled. May refer to the incoming lead time from suppliers, or to the order fulfillment lead time for you to get orders to customers.

Lean manufacturing: a collection of tools used to reduce waste and improve business processes.

Loading dock: a location for shipping and receiving materials, usually raised off the ground to allow for trucks to easily load and unload.

Materials Reserve: A designated amount of inventory that's kept for the purpose of being used after placing an order for re-stock. The reserve allows production to continue instead of stopping while more product is in shipment.

MOQ: Minimum Order Quantity. The lowest amount that a supplier will allow you to buy. Different suppliers have different MOQs.

Pack: The act of placing completed orders into shipping-ready containers such as boxes or pallets.

Pallet: A flat portable platform that can hold product to be moved. A manual pallet jack or forklift is often used to move pallets. The most common size is 40"x48" and is made of treated lumber.

Physical Inventory: refers to the management of stock levels, materials reserve, and other inventory in the studio using physical counts, physical signs, and moving items to different storage locations. Differs from virtual inventory, which manages such items on paper or on a computer.

Pick: the act of putting items together to fill a customer order. Picking usually includes using a packing slip or a pick list to check the order while the items are collected.

Pull: A system for reacting to a customer demand instead of a business forecast. A pull system means actions are performed only when triggered by a customer sale.

Push: The opposite of Pull. A system for pushing activities from a forecast or expectation rather than customer demand. Push systems should be avoided.

Red Tag: A method for identifying items that are out of place. Red tags can be placed on an item or out-of-place items can be moved to a storage location. Usually a red color is used to make it clear the item is not to be used for normal production.

Reorder Point: the inventory level at which a new order should be placed. Often used as another term for Materials Reserve.

Set in Order: The second step in the 5S process. Set in order finds a home for each item that belongs in an area.

Shine: The third step in the 5S process. Shine means to clean and maintain workstations and equipment.

Sort: The first step in the 5S process. Sorting removes all non-needed items from an area.

SOP: Standard Operating Procedure. An SOP documents the method for performing an action to help ensure it's done the same way each time.

Spaghetti Diagram: A method for drawing the path taken while performing an action. Drawing out the path taken allows you to see items that can be moved to make the layout of a process work better.

Standardize: The fourth step in the 5S process. Standardizing means that you add in cleaning and organizing steps into your regular procedures and regularly perform them in the same way.

Studio: Another word for workshop, factory, plant, etc – the place you make products.

Supplier: a business or person that provides a product or service.

Sustain: The fifth and last step in the 5S process. Sustain is committing to continue the 5S cycle for the long term to ensure a clean and organized studio.

TDS: Tech data sheet: A list of important features and properties of an item you purchase. Suppliers should provide these sheets on request.

Virtual Inventory: Methods for managing inventory without physically moving, labeling, or observing the item being inventoried. This can include using spreadsheets, notes, or software programs to check on inventory levels and determine when to reorder materials.

WIP: Work-In-Process: Items that have been transformed from their original state of raw materials and are not yet sellable finished goods. WIP might include batches of mixed ingredients or packaging that's labeled and waiting to be filled.

Work Cell: a location for performing a task. Called a cell because a relatively small round or square setup of about 5 by 5 feet is typical.

REFERENCES AND FURTHER READING

"Find Your next Commercial Property." *Commercial Real Estate*, 2019, www.loopnet.com/.

Identifying Waste on the Shopfloor. CRC Press, 2018.

5S For Operators: 5 Pillars of the Visual Workplace. Productivity Press, 1996.

Ching, Clarke. *The Bottleneck Rules: How to Get More Done (When Working Harder Isn't Working)*. 2018.

Gawande, Atul. *The Checklist Manifesto: How to Get Things Right*. Penguin Random House, 2014.

Goldratt, E. M., and John L. Cox. *The Goal*. Gower Publishing Company, Limited, 1993.

Fogg, BJ. "Tiny Habits." *Tinyhabits*, www.tinyhabits.com/.

Kanban for the Shopfloor. Productivity Press, 2002.

Boyd, Kenneth. *Cost Accounting For Dummies*. John Wiley & Sons, 2013.